萬曆

那些年

Years of Wanli

深圳市南山博物馆 编

文物出版社

万历文物主题特展

Special Exhibition on Artifacts of Wanli Reign

"万历那些年——万历文物主题特展"展览委员会

图录编辑

主　　编：戚　鑫　孙小兵
编　　委：黄海滨　冯雪　王钒
内容整理：王　钒
文字校对：王　钒　邓正榆　王思怡

展览组织与实施

深圳市南山博物馆团队

总策划：戚　鑫
展览统筹：黄海滨
展览策划：黄海滨　王　钒
展览执行：王　钒
展览协助：邓正榆
展陈设计：方丹霞　章慧玲
视觉设计：林洁纯　陈思敏
宣传推广：刘佳妮　余秀清　陈洁莹　黄旖旎　陈沫霖
社会教育：刘佳妮　白之仑　邱　烨　刘晏鑫　刘　娜
展品管理：王　钒　郑　宇　方楚瑜
展览摄影：林洁纯　王思怡

中国文物交流中心团队

总策划：谭　平
展览统筹：孙小兵　冯雪
展览策划：冯雪
展览执行：祁　钰　王宴姝　畅　言　许雅璐
摄　　影：杨　森

Exhibition Committee of "Years of Wanli - Special Exhibition on Artifacts of Wanli Reign"

Catalogue Editing

Chief Editor: Qi Xin, Sun Xiaobing
Editorial Board: Huang Haibin, Feng Xue, Wang Fan
Content Editor: Wang Fan
Proofreading: Wang Fan, Deng Zhengyu, Wang Siyi

Exhibition Organization and Implementation

Nanshan Museum

General Planning: Qi Xin
Exhibition Planning: Huang Haibin
Exhibition Curation: Huang Haibin, Wang Fan
Exhibition Production: Wang Fan
Exhibition Assistance: Deng Zhengyu
Exhibition Space Design: Fang Danxia, Zhang huiling
Exhibition Visual Design: Lin Jiechun, Chen Simin
Exhibition Promotion: Liu Jiani, Yu Xiuqing, Chen Jieying, Huang Yini, Chen Molin
Education & Public Programs: Liu Jiani, Bai Zhilun, Qiu Ye, Liu Yanxin, Liu Na
Objects Conservation: Wang Fan, Zheng Yu, Fang Chuyu
Exhibiton Photographer: Lin Jiechun, Wang Siyi

Art Exhibitions China

General Planning: Tan Ping
Exhibition Planning: Sun Xiaobing, Feng Xue
Exhibition Curation: Feng Xue
Exhibition Production: Qi Yu, Wang Yanshu, Chang Yan, Xu Yalu
Photographer: Yang Sen

参展单位及团队人员

北京市昌平区明十三陵管理中心
袁江玉　李慕禅　郑红艳
柏　宁　苏　静　曹新月
王雪峥

文化和旅游部恭王府博物馆
王东辉　孟庆重

国家文物局考古研究中心
唐　炜　孟原召　辛光灿
王亦晨　席光兰

中国文化遗产研究院

北京艺术博物馆
陈　静　张　巍　张振松
徐衍伟　杨俊艳　李　晔
杨小军　张　杰

Participating Institutions

Ming Tombs Administration Center

Yuan Jiangyu, Li Muchan, Zheng Hongyan,
Bai Ning, Su Jing, Cao Xinyue,
Wang Xuezheng

Prince Kung's Palace Museum

Wang Donghui, Meng Qingzhong

National Centre for Archaeology

Tang Wei, Meng Yuanzhao, Xin Guangcan,
Wang Yichen, Xi Guanglan

China Academy of Cultural Heritage

Beijing Art Museum

Chen Jing, Zhang Wei, Zhang Zhensong,
Xu Yanwei, Yang Junyan, Li Ye,
Yang Xiaojun, Zhang Jie

目录
Contents

前　言

　　万历，是明神宗朱翊钧的年号。朱翊钧是明朝的第十三位皇帝，通常以年号称其为万历皇帝。

　　定陵，是万历皇帝与孝端皇后、孝靖皇后的合葬墓，是我国第一座也是唯一一座被发掘的明代帝王陵。

　　隆庆六年 (1572 年)，朱翊钧登上皇位，至万历四十八年 (1620 年) 去世，在位共计 48 年，是明朝在位时间最长的皇帝。万历朝前十年，由张居正主政，厉行改革，气象一新。其后风波迭起，政治纷乱。与此同时，商品经济蓬勃发展，学术思想异常活跃，中西文化碰撞交流，文化艺术精彩纷呈。

　　本次展览以明定陵出土、水下考古发现及传世文物为支撑，以物叙事，以物证史。让我们透过这些承载着历史的文物，一起认识万历时代，品味独特的生活，欣赏精美的艺术，感受中国与世界的互动。

Wanli is the reign title of Emperor Shenzong, Zhu Yijun, the thirteenth emperor of the Ming Dynasty, commonly known as Wanli Emperor after his reign title.

Dingling Mausoleum is the mausoleum of Wanli Emperor and his two empresses, Empress Xiaoduan and Empress Xiaojing. It is the first and only imperial tomb of the Ming Dynasty excavated in China.

Zhu Yijun occupied the throne for 48 years from the sixth year of Longqing reign (1572) when he took the throne to his death in the 48th year of Wanli reign (1620), the longest among all the emperors in the Ming Dynasty. In the first decade of Wanli reign, the country put on a new look with a series reforms under Zhang Juzheng's administration. But it was soon followed by all kinds of disturbances and political turmoil. In the meantime, the empire witnessed a thriving commodity economy, a lively academic atmosphere, frequent cultural clashes and exchanges between China and the West, presenting a wonderful cultural and artistic landscape.

The exhibition focuses the narration and history on the artifacts unearthed from the Dingling Mausoleum of the Ming Dynasty, the underwater archaeological discoveries and the cultural relics handed down from the past. Let's learn about the Wanli reign, savor the unique life of the Ming people, appreciate the exquisite art and experience the interaction between China and the world through these cultural relics that bear the traces of history.

Foreword

明代帝王世系图（1368～1644年）

Genealogical Chart of the Ming Dynasty Emperors(1368 - 1644)

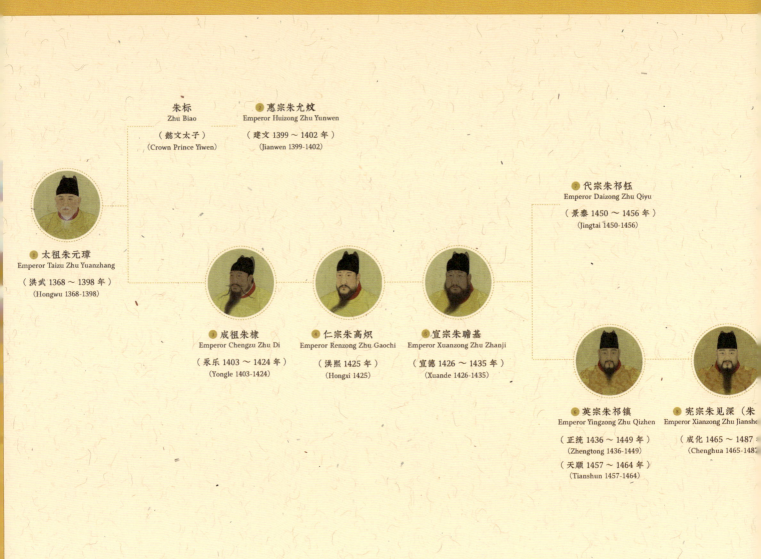

朱标
Zhu Biao

（懿文太子）
(Crown Prince Yiwen)

❷ 惠宗朱允炆
Emperor Huizong Zhu Yunwen

（建文 1399～1402 年）
(Jianwen 1399-1402)

❼ 代宗朱祁钰
Emperor Daizong Zhu Qiyu

（景泰 1450～1456 年）
(Jingtai 1450-1456)

❶ 太祖朱元璋
Emperor Taizu Zhu Yuanzhang

（洪武 1368～1398 年）
(Hongwu 1368-1398)

❸ 成祖朱棣
Emperor Chengzu Zhu Di

（永乐 1403～1424 年）
(Yongle 1403-1424)

❹ 仁宗朱高炽
Emperor Renzong Zhu Gaochi

（洪熙 1425 年）
(Hongxi 1425)

❺ 宣宗朱瞻基
Emperor Xuanzong Zhu Zhanji

（宣德 1426～1435 年）
(Xuande 1426-1435)

❻ 英宗朱祁镇
Emperor Yingzong Zhu Qizhen

（正统 1436～1449 年）
(Zhengtong 1436-1449)

（天顺 1457～1464 年）
(Tianshun 1457-1464)

❽ 宪宗朱见深（朱
Emperor Xianzong Zhu Jianshe

（成化 1465～1487
(Chenghua 1465-1487

⑨ 孝宗朱祐樘
Emperor Xiaozong Zhu Youcheng

（弘治 1488 ～ 1505 年）
(Hongzhi 1488-1505)

⑩ 武宗朱厚照
Emperor Wuzong Zhu Houzhao

（正德 1506 ～ 1521 年）
(Zhengde 1506-1521)

⑮ 熹宗朱由校
Emperor Xizong Zhu Youjiao

（天启 1621 ～ 1627 年）
(Tianqi 1621-1627)

朱祐杬
Zhu Youyuan

（兴献王）
(Prince Xingxian)

⑪ 世宗朱厚熜
Emperor Shizong Zhu Houcong

（嘉靖 1522 ～ 1566 年）
(Jiajing 1522-1566)

⑫ 穆宗朱载坖(朱载垕)
Emperor Muzong Zhu Zaiji (Zhu Zaihou)

（隆庆 1567 ～ 1572 年）
(Longqing 1567-1572)

⑬ 神宗朱翊钧
Emperor Shenzong Zhu Yijun

（万历 1573 ～ 1620 年）
(Wanli 1573-1620)

⑭ 光宗朱常洛
Emperor Guangzong Zhu Changluo

（泰昌 1620 年）
(Taichang 1620)

⑯ 思宗朱由检
Emperor Sizong Zhu Youjian

（崇祯 1628 ～ 1644 年）
(Chongzhen 1628-1644)

A Dynasty Standing

on Ceremony

中国是礼仪之邦，自周代以来，国家、社会、家族、文化等方方面面无不蕴含着"礼"的观念。明太祖朱元璋建立大明王朝伊始，为归统儒家礼制，革故鼎新，进行了自上而下的礼制规范。礼制引导着明朝的政治与社会秩序，约束着人们在社会生活、文化习俗、经济、外交等诸多领域的行为，对明代乃至后世社会都产生了深远影响。万历皇帝是位熟悉各种礼仪的君主，无论是冠礼成人、登基即位、祭祀天地宗庙，还是使臣觐见、朝会庆典，都遵循着各项礼仪制度的规范与典仪。

As a land of ceremony and propriety, China has been embedded with the notion of "etiquette" in the nation, society, family, and culture, among other aspects, since the Zhou Dynasty. In the early founding of the Ming Dynasty, Emperor Taizu Zhu Yuanzhang made a general reform to standardize the etiquette top-down to unify the Confucian system of rites. The rites and rituals exerted a profound impact on the Ming Dynasty and even later societies as a guide to the political and social order and a restriction on people's behaviors in social life, cultural customs, economy, and diplomacy of the Ming Dynasty. As a monarch familiar with various rituals, the Wanli Emperor followed the norms and rituals of various sets of etiquette, from entering adulthood, ascending to the throne, offering sacrifices to heaven and earth and ancestral temple, to receiving envoys and celebrating court gatherings.

第一单元

以礼

一　醉梦之朝

I. Overview of Wanli Reign

大明自洪武肇基，经永乐开拓，历仁宣之治，国力臻于鼎盛；正德、嘉靖之后开始衰落，万历朝时颓势愈显，遂有"明亡不在崇祯，而在万历"的论调。

隆庆六年（1572年）五月，明穆宗驾崩。同年六月，10岁的朱翊钧即位，次年改元万历。神宗即位之初，尚勤于政务，励精图治，全力支持新政，在首辅张居正的主持下，进行了政治、经济、军事等一系列改革。国家财政收入增加，边防稳固，整个社会欣欣向荣。但万历朝中后期，神宗怠于政事而耽于享乐，不郊不庙不朝近三十年，致使朝政昏怠、军备渐弛，社会矛盾不断激化，从而加速了明朝的衰亡。

The Great Ming developed to its heyday step by step from the early years of Hongwu Emperor and after the expansion of Yongle Emperor and the Rule of Renzong and Xuanzong; began to decline after Zhengde and Jiajing periods and met its downturn during the Wanli reign. So there is the saying "The Ming falls in Wanli not in Chongzhen".

In the fifth month of Longqing (1572), Emperor Muzong died. In the sixth month of the same year, the 10-year-old Zhu Yijun ascended the throne. In 1573, he changed his reign title to the first year of Wanli. Emperor Shenzong strived to make the nation strong and prosperous in the first years of his reign and carried out a series of reforms in politics, economy, and military affairs under the assistance of his Senior Grand Secretary Zhang Juzheng. The country thrived with its state revenue increased and the border defense strengthened. However, in the middle and later stages of the Wanli reign, Emperor Shenzong neglected his imperial role and indulged in pleasure, refused to offer sacrifices to heaven and earth, and ancestors, and refused to attend court meetings for nearly thirty years. The political and military affairs were overlooked and the social conflicts gradually intensified, thus accelerating the fall of the Ming Dynasty.

《大明集礼》

The Collection of Extended Rituals of Ming Dynasty

《大明集礼》是明朝唯一的通代礼典，洪武三年（1370 年）徐一夔等奉敕撰修，原本五十卷，上起尧舜，下至明代。嘉靖重修，增为五十三卷，除包括传统的吉、嘉、宾、军、凶五礼，又增加了冠服、车辂、仪仗、卤簿、字学、乐等内容，奠定了明朝礼制的基本格局。

The Collection of Extended Rituals of Ming Dynasty, the only general canon on rituals of the Ming Dynasty, was compiled by Xu Yikui and others in the third year of the Hongwu reign (1370) under the imperial edict. The original book had 50 volumes, covering the periods from Yao and Shun to the Ming Dynasty. During the reign of Emperor Jiajing, it was revised and expanded to 53 volumes, including not only the traditional five rites of Ji, Jia, Bin, Jun and Xiong, but also the contents of dressing codes, the standards of carriages and chariots, flags and weapons carried by guards of honor, Lubu, Zixue and music, forming the basic pattern of the Ming Dynasty's ritual system.

吉礼：祀天，祭地，宗庙，社稷，朝日、夕月，耤田享先农，专祀太岁、风、云、雷、雨师，专祀岳镇海渎、天下山川、城隍，祀旗纛，祀马祖、先牧、马社、马步，祭厉，祀典神祇，三皇，孔子。
（祭祀天神、地祇、人鬼的礼仪，为五礼之首）

Ji Li, or Sacrificial Rituals: Rites to offer sacrifices to heaven, earth, ancestral temples of the ruling house, the gods of land and grain, the rising of the sun and the moon, the god of agriculture, the gods of the year, the gods of wind, clouds, thunder and rain, the gods of mountains and rivers and sea, the god of town, the flags and banners, the horse breeding, the evils, the deities, the Three Emperors, and Confucius.
(Sacrificial rituals of offering sacrifices to heaven, earth, the living and the dead. The top of the Five Rites)

嘉礼：朝会，册拜，冠礼，婚礼，乡饮酒。
（朝会册拜、饮宴婚冠方面的礼仪）

Jia Li, or Festive Rites: Ceremonies for court meetings, conferment, capping for coming of age, marriage, drinking festivities in the district.
(Etiquettes related to court meetings, conferment, banquets, marriage and coming of age)

宾礼：朝贡，遣使。
（明朝与藩国往来的礼仪）

Bin Li, or Diplomatic Etiquettes: Rites concerning paying tribute to the court and dispatching envoys.
(Etiquettes of intercourse of Ming and its vassal states)

军礼：亲征，遣将，大射。
（军事活动方面的礼仪）

Jun Li, or Military Courtesies: Ceremonies for imperial personal expedition, for deployment of generals, and for holding imperial archery competitions.
(Rites related to military activities)

凶礼：吊赙，丧仪。
（凶丧有关的礼仪，丧葬和灾害等方面的礼仪）

Xiong Li, or Mourning Rites: Courtesies for contributing funeral expenses and mourning rites.
(Rites related to funeral arrangements, disastrous incidents, etc.)

冠礼成人

Capping Ceremony

隆庆六年（1572年）二月，明穆宗为十岁的朱翊钧举行了象征成人的冠礼。按照典制规定，他被引导进入殿前特设的帷帐，依次更换袍服、皮弁服、衮服，并分别佩戴翼善冠、皮弁冠、冕旒，是为"三加"之礼。而后出帷帐，着衮服，手持玉圭，举爵饮酒，跪听敕戒。在仪式的最后，他要祭祀先祖，拜谢皇上、皇后和皇贵妃。全部礼仪流程中，都有礼官唱导与教坊司奏乐。次日，他又被引导着端坐在殿前，接受百官庆贺。

In 2nd month, the 6th year of Longqing reign (1572), Emperor Muzong of Ming held a capping ceremony for his 10-year-old son Zhu Yijun as a symbol of his coming of age. According to the laws and institutions, he was guided into a special drapery set in the front of the palace to change into different robes and crown hats three times in succession, namely robe and *Yishan* crown hat, *Pibian* costume and *Pibian* crown hat, and *Gunfu* and *Mianliu*, known as the rite of "*San Jia* (Three Capping)". Then he walked out of the drapery in *Gunfu*, holding a jade *Gui* in both hands, raising a *Jue* (wine vessel), drinking the wine, and kneeling to listen to the imperial instructions. At the end of the ceremony, he offered sacrifices to his ancestors and thanked the emperor, empress, and imperial noble consort. The whole process was pre-announced by a master of ceremonies and accompanied by music played by the imperial music office. The day after, he was guided to sit in the front of the palace again to receive congratulations from the civil and military officials.

明代玉圭
Jade *Gui* of Ming Dynasty

玉圭，中国古代礼玉之一，形制有平首和尖首之分，平首圭可能源于原始人的生产工具——斧，逐渐演化为礼器；尖首圭则可能源于古代兵器——戈，象征权力和力量。明代，玉圭成为皇室礼服的重要组成部分，用来象征尊贵。依万历《大明会典》所记，洪武六年定，亲王朝觐天子，先穿常服、行家礼，再穿冕服、行君臣之礼，行君臣礼时，天子要执传位大圭，上刻"奉天法祖，世世相传"，以正君臣之位。

Jade *Gui* is a kind of ritual jade in ancient China. In terms of shape and structure, it can be divided into flat-top *Gui* and pointed-top *Gui*. The former is likely to have originated from the axe - a production tool of primitive people, which gradually evolved into a ritual object; the latter could be derived from an ancient weapon – *Ge* (dagger-axe), symbolizing power and strength. In the Ming Dynasty, jade *Gui* became an important component of the imperial ceremonial costume to symbolize dignity. According to the records of *Collected Statutes of the Ming Dynasty (Da Ming Hui Dian)* in Wanli reign, as stipulated in the sixth year of Hongwu's reign, when the Crown Prince had an audience with the emperor, he should first observe the family rituals in regular attire and then perform the courtesy as a subject to the monarch in *Mian* costume, and the emperor should hold the Grand *Gui* to his heir, which inscribed with the characters "In the name of gods and ancestors, pass it down generation after generation", in order to justify the positions of the ruler and his subject.

明定陵出土玉圭
Jade *Gui* unearthed from the Dingling Mausoleum of Ming Dynasty

玉脊圭

明万历
北京市昌平区明十三陵定陵出土
长 26.8、宽 5.9、厚 0.9 厘米
明十三陵博物馆藏

Jade ridged *Gui*

Wanli reign of Ming Dynasty

Unearthed from the Dingling Mausoleum of the Ming Tombs
in Changping District, Beijing

Length 26.8 cm, Width 5.9 cm, Thickness 0.9 cm

The Ming Tombs Museum

明定陵出土玉圭共 8 件，其中 4 件出自万历帝棺
内西端胸前，4 件出自随葬器物箱内。

这件玉圭出土时放在长方形漆匣内。圭为白玉制
成，正面中间有脊，两侧各有一道凹槽，槽内突起一
条抹角圆棱或谓"双植纹"，定名为"脊圭"。《大
明会典》记载天子皮弁服玉圭："圭长如冕服之圭，
有脊，并双植文。"左右两条竖纹表示"双植"，中
间一条则为"脊"，双植纹从平面来看，也可解释为
两组四条阴刻竖线，每两条阴线构成一个凸条纹，是
为代表桓楹的两个竖柱，即双植。

A total of 8 jade *Gui* were unearthed from the Dingling Mausoleum,
of which 4 were from Wanli Emperor's chest in the west of the coffin
and 4 were from the boxes of the burial objects.

This piece was found in a rectangular lacquer box at the time of
excavation. The *Gui* is made of white jade, carved with a ridge
in the middle of the front and a groove on either side, where
protrudes a rounded edge, known as "double-pillar design", so
it is named "Ridged *Gui*". As recorded in the *Collected Statutes
of the Ming Dynasty (Da Ming Hui Dian)* that the emperor's jade
Gui of his *Pibian* costume, "The *Gui* is as long as the *Gui* of the
Mian costume. It has a ridge and double-pillar design." The two
vertical lines on the left and right represent "double pillars", while
the middle line represents "ridge". From a plane perspective,
the double-pillar design can also be interpreted as two sets of
four incised vertical lines, each of the two lines forms a convex,
representing the two vertical pillars, namely double pillars.

明代玉璧
Jade *Bi* Disc of Ming Dynasty

明代的统治阶级出于稳定社会、安定人心的目的，提出"法先王"的政治口号，因此大量制作与《周礼》规定有关的礼玉，故在元代曾一度衰落的礼器，如璧、琮、圭等，又重新出现，但仿古风格明显。

明代属于我国经济高度繁荣的历史时期之一，这一时期玉器品种多、质量佳、雕琢精、用途广，在中国玉文化史上占有重要地位。明代玉器风格清新、刚劲、棱角分明，具有较高的艺术与审美价值。明代雕玉工艺有浮雕、透雕等，雕刻技法粗犷浑厚，镂空技法使用普遍。

明代早期纹饰总体风格趋于简练豪放，多以龙凤花鸟为主要题材，雕琢工艺简练浑厚圆润；中期渐向纤巧、细腻的方向发展，花卉题材多采用折枝和缠枝花卉组成图案，清新活泼，在工艺上趋向玲珑复杂；到了晚期，风格趋于繁复，出现分层镂雕手法，显得玲珑剔透。

The ruling class of the Ming Dynasty proposed the political slogan of "Following the examples of the previous sovereigns" to maintain social order and reassure the public, so they produced a large number of ritual jade pieces related to the provisions of the *Rites of Zhou (Zhou Li)*. Therefore, ritual objects such as *Bi*, *Cong*, and *Gui* that had once declined in the Yuan Dynasty reappeared, mostly modeling after the ancient styles.

The Ming Dynasty was one of the historical periods in China with a highly prosperous economy. During this period, jade ware with great variety, good quality and exquisite carving was used extensively, occupying an important position in the history of Chinese jade culture. The jade ware of the Ming Dynasty had high artistic and aesthetic value with its fresh, vigorous style and distinctive edges and corners. Jade carving crafts included relief and openwork, showing robust and vigorous carving techniques, among which openwork techniques prevailed.

The overall style of decorative patterns in the early Ming Dynasty tended to be concise and bold, themed mainly on dragons, phoenixes, flowers and birds, and the carving techniques were simple, mellow and round; the style gradually developed towards a delicate and smooth and fine direction in the middle period, with floral themes often composed of design of plucked and interlocking branches of flowers, which were fresh and lively. The craftsmanship tended to be exquisite and complicated; in the late Ming, sophistication and the layered hollow carving techniques became the fashion, looking artful and exquisite.

玉璧经典谷纹
Jade *Bi* with classic grain pattern

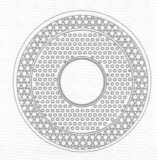

玉璧经典蒲纹
Jade *Bi* with classic rush mat pattern

明代玉璧上的盘凤蒲纹
Jade *Bi* with twisted phoenix design and rush mat pattern in the Ming Dynasty

（出自《中国经典纹样图鉴》）
(Source: *The Chinese Classic Pattern Book*)

玉璧（2件）

明万历
北京市昌平区明十三陵定陵出土
直径 7.76、厚 0.74 厘米；直径 7.8、厚 0.7 厘米
明十三陵博物馆藏

Jade *Bi* disc (2 pcs)

Wanli reign of Ming Dynasty

Unearthed from the Dingling Mausoleum of the Ming Tombs
in Changping District, Beijing

Diameter 7.76 cm, Thickness 0.74 cm

Diameter 7.8 cm, Thickness 0.7 cm

The Ming Tombs Museum

冠冕服带

Imperial Costumes and Crown Hats

万历《大明会典》记载，明朝皇帝冠服以衮冕服等级最高，是皇帝祭祀天地、宗庙、社稷、先农，以及正旦、冬至、圣节、册拜时服用的礼服。其制由冕冠、玉圭、衮服、大带、革带、玉佩、蔽膝、绶、中单、朱袜、赤舄相配。除典制中记载的上衣下裳形制的衮服外，明代还有一种袍式的衮服，同样饰有日、月、星辰、山、龙、华虫、宗彝、藻、火、粉米、黼、黻十二章图案。定陵出土的五件万历帝衮服均属袍式衮服，其中刺绣三件、缂丝两件，所配冠为翼善冠而非冕。

Based on the records of *Collected Statutes of the Ming Dynasty*, the *Gunfu* and *Mian* crown hat are the top-grade ceremonial costumes for Ming emperors, who wore them on ceremonial occasions such as offering sacrifices to heaven and earth, ancestral temples, gods of the land and grain, god of agriculture, as well as on the New Year's Day, the Winter Solstice, emperor's birthday and on the days of conferment. The whole set consists of a crown hat, a jade *Gui*, a *Gunfu* (robes worn by the emperor), a large sash, a leather belt, a jade pendant, a pair of knee covers, a ribbon, underwear, a pair of red socks and a pair of red shoes. In addition to the *Gunfu* with top and skirt recorded in the book, there was also a type of robe-style imperial attire in the Ming Dynasty, adorned with twelve imperial symbols representing sun, moon, constellation, mountain, dragon, pheasant, two ritual vessels, waterweed, fire, grains, axe and a device of doubtful origin (*Fu*). The five *Gunfu* of Wanli Emperor unearthed from the Dingling Mausoleum are all robe-style attires, including three embroidered pieces and two silk tapestry pieces, matched with *Yishan* crown hats rather than *Mian* crown hats.

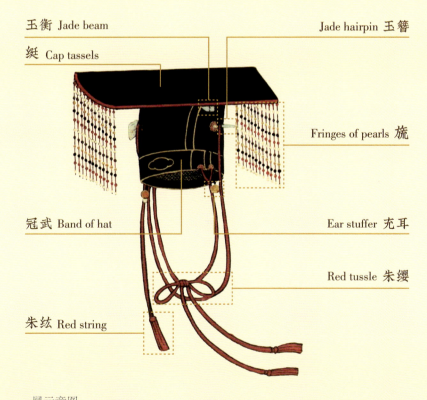

冕示意图

Illustrations of a *Mian* crown hat

玉衡 Jade beam
綖 Cap tassels
Jade hairpin 玉簪
Fringes of pearls 旒
冠武 Band of hat
Ear stuffer 充耳
Red tussle 朱纩
朱纮 Red string

十二章纹

Twelve Imperial Symbols

十二章纹，是中国古代服饰等级标志，指中国古代帝王及高级官员礼服上绘绣的十二种纹饰，分别是：日、月、星辰、山、龙、华虫、宗彝、藻、火、粉米、黼、黻等，通称"十二章"，绘绣有章纹的礼服称为"章服"。十二章纹包含了至善至美的帝德，象征皇帝是大地的主宰，其权力"如天地之大，万物涵复载之中，如日月之明，八方围照临之内"。

The twelve imperial symbols embroidered on imperial dragon robes conventionally represent the sun, the moon, a constellation, a mountain, the dragon, the pheasant, two ritual vessels, waterweed, fire, grains, an axe, and *Fu* (a device of doubtful origin). The emperor wore all twelve, other persons wore only those appropriate to their rank. The twelve imperial symbols imply the supreme good and supreme beauty of the emperor as the ruler under heaven, whose power is "as great as heaven and earth, encompassing all things in the universe; as bright as the sun and moon, illuminating all corners of the world".

日，月，星辰
Sun, moon, and constellation

华虫
Pheasant

山
Mountain

龙
Dragon

宗彝
Two ritual vessels

藻
Waterweed

火
Fire

粉米
Grains

黼
Axe

黻
Fu

黄缂丝十二章福寿如意衮服
Yellow silk tapestry *Gunfu* (robes worn by the emperor) embroidered with twelve imperial symbols

十二章的含义
The meaning of the twelve imperial symbols

日、月、星辰：称为"三光"，取其"照临"之意，昼夜有光，普照天下。

Sun, moon, and constellation: the sun, moon, and constellation are known as the "three lights", meaning there is light day and night, illuminating all over the world.

山：取"镇"土之意，能行云雨，人所仰望。

Mountain: solid and stable, and can withhold clouds and rain, is something people look up to.

龙：取"变化无方"，取其神。

Dragon: mystical and changeable, taking for its spirit.

华虫：是雉鸡，翎毛华美，表示"文采昭著"，取其文。

Pheasant: with beautiful feathers, indicating "outstanding literary talent".

宗彝：为宗庙祭器，一为虎，取其严猛；一为蜼，长尾猴，取其智慧。

Two ritual vessels: one is a tiger, for its fierceness; the other is a long-tailed monkey, for its wisdom.

藻：是有花纹的水草，取其有"文"，其"洁"。

Waterweed: for its "erudition (*wen*, the grass pattern)" and "cleanness".

火：即火焰，取其"明亮"。

Fire: for its "blaze and bright".

粉米：是粮食，人离不开米面，取义养人。

Grains: implying food that can sustain people.

黼：是斧头的形状，取义"果断""权威"。

Axe: implying "decisive" and "authoritative".

黻：是两个弓相背，取臣民背恶向善之意，亦取君臣离合去就之理。

Fu: two bows back-to-back, implying people turn away from evil and follow virtue or the distance and proper behaviors between the monarch and his subjects.

黄缂丝十二章福寿如意衮服（复制品）

明万历
北京市昌平区明十三陵定陵出土
袖长 232、下摆宽 174、身长 133、袖宽 55、
袖口宽 18 厘米
明十三陵博物馆藏

Yellow silk tapestry *Gunfu* embroidered with twelve imperial symbols (replica)

Wanli reign of Ming Dynasty

Unearthed from the Dingling Mausoleum of the Ming Tombs in Changping District, Beijing

Length of Sleeve 232 cm, Width of Hem 174 cm, Body Length 133 cm, Width of Sleeve 55 cm, Width of Cuff 18 cm

The Ming Tombs Museum

　　万历帝服饰。通体缂制而成，地纹缂"卍""寿"字、蝙蝠和如意云纹，象征"万寿洪福"。十二团龙分别缂制在前后身及两袖部位，每一团龙又单独构成一组圆形图案，中心为一条蛟龙，两侧为"八吉祥"纹样。蛟龙之上再饰流云，龙下饰海水江崖。"八吉祥"纹是八种图案纹样，即轮、罗、伞、盖、花、罐、鱼、盘长。在十二团龙图案之外，又缂十二章纹样，这就是属于帝王特有的十二章衮服。

　　此为 1983 年南京云锦研究所复制。

Robe of Wanli Emperor. The whole piece is carved silk, with the ground carved with the design of the characters "卍 寿 (*Wan and Shou*)", bats and Ruyi-sceptre designs, symbolizing "longevity and great blessing". Twelve dragon roundels are carved on the front, back, and two sleeves. Each dragon roundel forms a separate circular pattern, with a sea dragon in the center and the eight Buddhist emblems of good augur on either side. The sea dragon is adorned with the design of flowing clouds above and stylized waves and mountain peaks below. The eight Buddhist emblems are the design of a wheel, a white conch shell, a parasol, an endless knot, a lotus, a treasure vase, a pair of fish, and a victory banner. The Gunfu is carved with the Twelve Imperial Symbols in addition to the twelve dragon roundels, dedicated especially to the emperor.

This is a reproduction of Nanjing Yunjin Brocade Research Institute in 1983.

绛红织金寿字妆花缎衬褶袍（复制品）

明万历
北京市昌平区明十三陵定陵出土
袖长 231、下摆宽 154、身长 132、袖宽 51、
袖口宽 17.5 厘米
明十三陵博物馆藏

Pleated robe with crimson satin woven with the design of golden *"Shou* (longevity)" characters (replica)

Wanli reign of Ming Dynasty

Unearthed from the Dingling Mausoleum of the Ming Tombs in Changping District, Beijing

Length of Sleeve 231 cm, Width of Hem 154 cm, Body Length 132 cm, Width of Sleeve 51 cm, Width of Cuff 17.5 cm

The Ming Tombs Museum

万历帝服饰。地纹为灵芝捧金"寿"字、仙鹤托金"寿"字，主纹上衣部分为龙云肩通绣柿蒂形，下裳部分有龙襕，上饰龙戏珠、海水、江崖、祥云等，均为金线绞边。

Robe of Wanli Emperor. The ground is woven with design of *Lingzhi* (a glossy ganoderma) and crane holding the golden *"Shou* (longevity)" characters. The top is the persimmon calyx pattern with the design of dragons and clouds on the shoulders; the lower garment has a dragon band decorated with dragons playing with a pearl, stylized waves and mountain peaks, S-shaped clouds, etc., all of which have twined edges of golden thread.

翼善冠示意图
Illustrations of *Yishan* crown hat

金二龙戏珠
Gold two dragons
playing with a pearl

系结系带
Buckles

折角
Rabbit ears

后山
Back mountain

永乐三年更定，冠以乌纱冒之，折角向上，其后名翼善冠。

It was reformulated in the 3rd year of Yongle reign that the hats made of black gauze were to have rabbit ears,
later with the name of *Yishan* Crown Hat.

——《明史 · 舆服志》

- History of Ming: Carriage and Costumes

乌纱翼善冠（复制品）

明万历
北京市昌平区明十三陵定陵出土
通高 26.5、帽径 19 厘米
明十三陵博物馆藏

Yishan crown hat made of black gauze (replica)

Wanli reign of Ming Dynasty

Unearthed from the Dingling Mausoleum of the Ming Tombs in Changping District, Beijing

Overall Height 26.5 cm, Diameter of Hat 19 cm

The Ming Tombs Museum

冠用细竹丝编成六角形网格状纹作胎，后山前面嵌二龙戏珠，龙身为金累丝编结制成，每条龙上嵌有宝石和珍珠，中有金火焰一个。下部为金质扁筒形插座，正面浮雕有升龙，三山形。龙首托字，一为"万"字，一为"寿"字。背面饰云纹。

The crown hat is made on the body of a hexagonal grid pattern woven with fine bamboo strings. The front of the back mountain is embedded with two dragons playing with a pearl. The dragon body is stranded welding of gold wires, and each dragon is inlaid with gemstones and pearls, with a golden fire of flames in the middle. The lower part is a gold flat cylindrical receptacle, with a rising dragon and three mountains in relief on the front. There are two characters above the head of the two dragons, one is "*Wan*" and the other is "*Shou*" (together meaning long life). The back is decorated with cloud design.

金翼善冠（复制品）

明万历
北京市昌平区明十三陵定陵出土
通高 24.5、帽径 16.9~18.3 厘米
明十三陵博物馆藏

Gold *Yishan* crown hat (replica)

Wanli reign of Ming Dynasty
Unearthed from the Dingling Mausoleum of the Ming Tombs
in Changping District, Beijing
Overall Height 24.5 cm, Diameter of Hat 16.9 - 18.3 cm
The Ming Tombs Museum

　　金冠全部用金丝编结而成，共 852 根极细的 0.2
毫米金丝，结构复杂，制作精细，孔眼匀称，外表不
露接头痕迹，薄如轻纱。半圆形的帽山上挺立着两个
像兔耳形状的金丝网片，这部分叫做"金折角"。金
冠上镶嵌了两条左右对称的盘龙，盘龙中间镶嵌一枚
火珠，构成二龙戏珠的图案。这两条金龙造型生动有力，
气势雄伟，是金冠的点睛之笔，也是金冠制作中复杂
的部分。

　　金冠制作采用了掐丝、累丝、码丝、焊接等多种
工艺，是充分反映明代金银制作工艺最高水平的杰作，
目前在我国只此一顶，也是迄今为止我国现存唯一一
顶帝王金冠。

The crown hat is woven entirely with gold wires, using 852
extremely fine gold wires of 0.2 mm. The hat is as thin as gauze,
with a complicated structure, exquisite craftsmanship, and uniform
mesh holes, showing no trace of joint marks from the outlook.
Two gold wire mesh pieces in the shape of rabbit ears erect on the
semicircular mountain on the back of the hat, known as "rabbit
ears". The hat is also inlaid with two symmetrical coiled dragons
and a pearl in the middle, a motif of two dragons playing with a
pearl. The two gold dragons looking vivid and powerful in shape
and magnificent in momentum are the finishing touch of the gold
mesh crown, also the sophisticated part of the technology in the hat
making.

A variety of crafts were adopted to make the gold crown hat,
including filigree, stranded welding, wire stacking, soldering,
which fully reflected the highest level of gold and silver production
technology in the Ming Dynasty. It is the only imperial gold crown
hat found in China so far.

腰带与带钩

Belts and Belt Hooks

明代的腰带饰玉有钩环、带扣、带穿、挂环、带钩等。玉带钩是明代最常见的玉带饰，它在战国早期开始流行，种类多样。从使用来看，带钩主要分为两种，一种为横钩，用来系结绦带；另一种是纵钩，使用时钩头向下，钩挂其他物品。明代玉带钩的使用受到传统玉器的影响，亦分为横钩及纵钩两种，横钩主要用于结带，纵向使用的钩是挂钩。

The jade belt in the Ming Dynasty had hooks and loops, belt buckles, belt loops, hanging rings and belt hooks. Jade belt hook was the most common jade belt decoration in the Ming Dynasty, and its popularity can be traced in the early the Warring States period, and with a variety of types. From the perspective of usage, there are mainly two types of belt hooks: one is the horizontal hook, which is used to tie the ribbon; another is the vertical hook, to hang things with its hook tip downward. Influenced by traditional jade ware, the Ming Dynasty also used jade belt with horizontal hooks and vertical hooks, with the former for tying the belt, and the latter for hanging.

大碌带

明万历
北京市昌平区明十三陵定陵出土
通长 138、宽 6.2 厘米
明十三陵博物馆藏

The emerald belt (*Da Lu* belt)

Wanli reign of Ming Dynasty
Unearthed from the Dingling Mausoleum of the Ming Tombs
in Changping District, Beijing
Overall Length 138 cm, Width 6.2 cm
The Ming Tombs Museum

　　万历帝服饰。束带是明代制服的重要佩饰，自皇帝而下，王公贵族、文武百官依品职佩戴不同束带。这条束带用料珍贵，装饰华丽，是万历皇帝的心爱之物。它的制作十分精美，用双层黄色素缎，内夹一层皮革制成。大碌带上共缝缀了 20 个缠枝花形金托，上面镶嵌有祖母绿、红宝石和珍珠，显得异常华丽。背面镂雕金龙图案，工艺十分精湛。据出土报告统计，带上共有祖母绿 20 块，石榴子红宝石 91 块，其中体积最大、价值最高的是祖母绿。祖母绿属绿柱石类，颜色与翡翠相似，产于西伯利亚、巴基斯坦等地，价格昂贵。金饰件上所嵌珍珠绝大多已腐朽不存。考古学家们根据带下绢条墨书题记："宝藏库取来大碌带"字样，故名"大碌带"。目前为止，此种款式的玉带，仅发现一条。专家认为，大碌带是万历皇帝在重大场合时佩戴的束带，在明朝玉带的基础上演化而来，上面镶嵌宝石的形状和数量，也参照明朝有关的服饰制度要求制作而成。

Costume of Wanli Emperor. Girdle, or belt, was an important accessory of garments in the Ming Dynasty, worn differently by the emperor, princes, and nobles, as well as civil and military officials according to their official ranks. The Emerald Belt made of precious materials and adorned gorgeously was a cherished treasure of Wanli Emperor. It was exquisitely crafted by wrapping a layer of leather with two layers of yellow satin. It is sewn with 20 gold holders in the shape of interlocking branches and flowers, inlaid with emeralds, rubies, and pearls, looking exceedingly gorgeous. The back is hollow-carved with the design of golden dragons, demonstrating exquisite craftsmanship. According to the excavation report, there are a total of 20 emeralds and 91 garnet rubies on the belt, of which the largest and most valuable is emerald. Emerald belongs to the beryl class, with a color similar to jadeite. Produced in Siberia, Pakistan, and other places, it is highly valued. Most of the pearls embedded in gold ornaments have decayed and disappeared. Archaeologists named it "The Emerald Belt" based on the ink scripts on the silk strip below the belt: "Take out the *Da Lu* belt from the treasure trove". It is by far the only jade belt of such style discovered. Experts believe that the Emerald Belt was worn by Wanli Emperor on important occasions and evolved from the jade belt of the Ming Dynasty. The shape and quantity of the inlaid gemstones on it were also made in accordance with the requirements of relevant costume system of the Ming Dynasty.

背面
The Back

白玉带钩

明万历
北京市昌平区明十三陵定陵出土
长 14.2、宽 2.5 厘米
明十三陵博物馆藏

White jade belt hook

Wanli reign of Ming Dynasty
Unearthed from the Dingling Mausoleum of the Ming Tombs
in Changping District, Beijing
Length 14.2 cm, Width 2.5 cm
The Ming Tombs Museum

　　带钩雕作龙首形，背部有一椭圆形钮，龙首颈项两侧、颈后阴刻三绺一组发绺。龙嘴吻部齐平，张口，口内雕琢有上翘龙舌，吻部上下两对长牙相对。带钩共镶嵌 7 颗宝石，龙额金托镶嵌绿宝石 1 颗。龙睛各嵌 1 颗猫睛石（猫眼石），1 颗已佚。龙腹金托镶嵌 4 颗宝石，依次是黄宝石、红宝石、蓝宝石、红宝石。

The belt hook is carved in the shape of a dragon's head with an oval button on the back. Three hair locks are incised on either side and back of the dragon's neck. The dragon's snout is flush, with its mouth open and carved with an upturned dragon tongue inside. The upper and lower pairs of long teeth on the snout face each other. The belt hook is inlaid with 7 gemstones, and an emerald is embedded on the gold holder of the dragon's forehead. The dragon's eyes are inlaid with a cat's-eye stone each, but one is missing. Four gemstones of a topaz, a ruby, a sapphire and a ruby are inlaid in turn on the gold holders of the dragon belly.

凤冠霞帔

Phoenix Crown and Embroidered Tasseled Cape

明代后妃服饰由朝、祭所用的礼服与燕居所用的常服组成。据万历《大明会典》记载，永乐三年（1405 年）更定皇后礼服为九龙四凤冠、翟衣、中单、蔽膝、玉榖圭、玉革带、大带、绶、玉佩、青袜舄（xì）。皇后常服则为双凤翊龙冠、大衫、霞帔、鞠衣、四襈袄子、大带、缘襈袄子、缘襈裙、玉带、玉花采结绶、青袜舄。其中霞帔以狭长丝罗制作，是身份等级的象征。穿着时佩挂于颈，由领后绕至胸前，下垂至膝，底部悬挂坠子。除皇后常服外，霞帔也用作妃嫔、公主、命妇的礼服，依等级不同而织纹有别，坠子的材质也各不相同。

In the Ming Dynasty, the costumes of the empress and consorts consisted of ceremonial attire for ritual occasions and regular attire at leisure. According to the records of *Collected Statutes of the Ming Dynasty*, it was reformulated in the 3rd year of Yongle reign that the empress' ceremonial attire should include a crown of nine dragons and four phoenixes, *Zhaiyi* (a robe embroidered with long-tail pheasant), underwear, a pair of knee covers, a jade *Gui*, a jade belt, a big sash, a ribbon, a jade pendant, and a pair of green socks and shoes. The empress' regular attire should consist of a dragon crown with double phoenixes, a long gown, an embroidered tasseled cape, *Juyi* (a mulberry leaf-colored dress), a coat decorated with strip rims, a large sash, a jacket decorated with strip rims, a skirt decorated with strip rims, a jade belt, a ribbon, and a pair of green socks and shoes. Among them, the cape is made of silk tassels as a symbol of status and rank. It is worn around the neck from the back of the neck to the front of the chest, drooping down to the knees, with pendants hanging at the bottom of the cape. The cape is also part of the formal dress for consorts and concubines, princesses, and noble ladies, with different weaving patterns and varied materials of pendants based on their ranks.

龙凤冠

Dragon and Phoenix Crown

龙凤冠是皇后的礼冠，在受册、谒庙或者朝会时戴用。古代皇后的服装非常讲究，常有"凤冠霞帔"的说法，实际上，凤冠霞帔是所有皇后、妃嫔、命妇用于朝见等礼仪场合的礼服统称，细分起来等级差别严格。明代凤冠有两种形制，一种是后妃所服，冠上除缀凤凰外，还有龙、翚（huī）等装饰。另一种是命妇所戴的彩冠，上面不缀龙凤仅缀珠翠、花钗。明定陵出土有四顶皇后龙凤冠，分别为孝端皇后的九龙九凤冠、六龙三凤冠和孝靖皇后的十二龙九凤冠、三龙二凤冠。四顶龙凤冠所用饰件与制度均不完全相符。

The Dragon and Phoenix Crown is a ceremonial crown worn by the empress when receiving conferment, visiting ancestral temples, or attending court meetings. The attire of ancient empresses was very particular, often known as the term "phoenix crown and tasseled cape". Actually, the term was the umbrella term for the ceremonial attire of empresses, consorts and concubines, and noble ladies on ritual occasions such as court meetings, which could be vastly different if subdivided according to a strict hierarchy. In the Ming Dynasty, there were two forms of phoenix crowns. One was worn by empresses, which was adorned with dragons and pheasants besides phoenixes. Another type was the colorful crown worn by noble ladies, which was not adorned with dragons and phoenixes, but only with pearl and flower hairpins. Four empress' crowns were unearthed from the Dingling Mausoleum. They were respectively Empress Xiaoduan's crown with nine dragons and nine phoenixes and crown with six dragons and three phoenixes as well as Empress Xiaojing's crown with twelve dragons and nine phoenixes and crown with three dragons and two phoenixes. The four crowns are not entirely the same in terms of ornaments and structure.

十二龙九凤冠（复制品）

明万历
北京市昌平区明十三陵定陵出土
通高 28、帽径 32 厘米
明十三陵博物馆藏

Crown decorated with twelve dragons and nine phoenixes (replica)

Wanli reign of Ming Dynasty

Unearthed from the Dingling Mausoleum of the Ming Tombs in Changping District, Beijing

Overall Height 28 cm, Diameter of Hat 32 cm

The Ming Tombs Museum

孝靖后凤冠。冠上饰十二龙九凤，龙以花丝制作，凤点翠。一眼望去，凤冠上金龙升腾奔跃在翠云之上，翠凤飞翔在珠宝花叶之中，龙凤口衔接珠宝串饰，珠光宝气交相辉映，美不胜收。

Crown of Empress Xiaojing. The crown is adorned with twelve dragons and nine phoenixes. The dragons are made of filigree and inlaid with phoenixes. At a glance, the gold dragons on the crown soar and leap above the emerald clouds, and the emerald phoenixes fly among the gemmed flowers and leaves. Both the dragons and phoenixes hold jade pendants in their mouths, glistening with jewels, extremely beautiful.

霞帔坠

明万历
北京市昌平区明十三陵定陵出土
通高 17.1、柄长 17.7 厘米
明十三陵博物馆藏

Cape pendant

Wanli reign of Ming Dynasty

Unearthed from the Dingling Mausoleum of the Ming Tombs in Changping District, Beijing

Overall Height 17.1 cm, Length of Pin 17.7 cm

The Ming Tombs Museum

　　器身为桃形，顶部以金链与花托形四叶相连，上端再以金链与带钩形提梁相系，器身两侧分别镂刻二龙戏珠及海水江崖和云纹。一侧中部嵌珍珠一颗，四叶用金丝掐制成细密的叶脉纹，中心嵌红、蓝宝石。

　　根据明代的服制，霞帔是后妃、命妇穿着的重要礼仪服饰，霞帔坠则是用来固定霞帔的器物。帔坠的基本形状是中空，左右两半分制而成，扣合在一起呈桃形，多伴有挂钩。帔坠材质多为金、鎏金或银质，纹饰多以镂空錾刻的禽鸟纹为主，亦有龙纹和花卉纹等。

The pendant has a peach-shaped body and its top is connected to the four flower-holder-shaped leaves through a gold chain. The upper end is connected with the gold chain and a hoop handle. On either side of the body, it is respectively carved with the design of two dragons playing with a pearl, and stylized waves and mountain peaks and clouds. One pearl is embedded in the middle of one side, and the four leaves are made of fine vein patterns with golden filigree, and inlaid with rubies and sapphires in the center.

According to the costume system of the Ming Dynasty, the tasseled cape was an important ceremonial attire worn by empresses and noble women, while the cape pendants were used to fix the cape. Usually, the cape pendant is hollow, with the left and right parts made separately and fitted together in a peach shape and often with a hook. The materials of the cape pendants are mostly gold, gilt, or silver, and the decorative patterns, are mainly hollow carved bird patterns, dragon patterns and floral patterns.

绿织金妆花缎立领女夹衣（复制品）

明万历
北京市昌平区明十三陵定陵出土
袖长 240、下摆宽 88、身长 83、袖宽 53、
袖口宽 22.5 厘米
明十三陵博物馆藏

Woman's lined dress with standing collar
(replica)

Wanli reign of Ming Dynasty

Unearthed from the Dingling Mausoleum of the Ming Tombs
in Changping District, Beijing

Length of Sleeve 240 cm, Width of Hem 88 cm, Body Length
83 cm, Width of Sleeve 53 cm, Width of Cuff 22.5 cm

The Ming Tombs Museum

孝端后服饰。以暗花升降龙戏珠、四季花卉纹为地，胸部为二龙戏珠纹，背部饰正面龙戏珠、海水、江崖、四季花卉、八宝纹。

Costume of Empress Xiaoduan. The ground is adorned with the design of two dragons playing with a pearl and flowers and plants. The front chest is adorned with the design of two dragons playing with a pearl, and the back is adorned with the design of stylized waves and mountain peaks, flowers and plants, and eight Buddhist emblems.

张居正像

Portrait of Zhang Juzheng

张居正像
（出自《张文忠公全集》）
Portrait of Zhang Juzheng
(Source: *The Complete Works of Zhang Wenzhong*)

张居正（1525～1582年），字叔大，湖广江陵（今湖北荆州）人，嘉靖二十六年（1547年）进士。明穆宗在位时，遗命高拱、张居正等三位大臣辅政。隆庆六年（1572年），张居正联合宦官冯保扳倒高拱，成为首辅。由于神宗年幼，国家大政实际由张居正裁决，他采取了一系列改革措施，成效卓著。《明史·张居正传》中对其评价道："肩劳任怨，举废饬弛，弼成万历初年之治。其时中外乂安，海内殷阜，纪纲法度，莫不修明。"

Zhang Juzheng (1525 - 1582), courtesy name Shuda, was born in Jiangling, Huguang (today's Jingzhou, Hubei). He became a *Jinshi* in the 26th year of Jiajing reign (1547). When Emperor Muzong of Ming was in reign, he ordered three ministers including Gao Gong and Zhang Juzheng to be the regency to assist his heir-apparent before his death. In the 6th year of Longqing reign (1572), allying with the eunuch Feng Bao, Zhang Juzheng removed Gao Gong from his office and became the Senior Grand Secretary. The young Emperor Shenzong relied heavily on Zhang Juzheng who held the actual power for state affairs. Zhang implemented a series of reform measures with remarkable results. He was commented on *History of Ming: Biography of Zhang Juzheng* as: "Shouldered great responsibilities, but never complained; carried out a series of reforms in the early years of Wanli reign. During that time, the economy and military power prospered and the laws and regulations were specified."

张居正不仅是首辅，还兼管万历的学习事务，为小皇帝任命主讲老师和侍读，亲自编绘教材、讲解经史。《帝鉴图说》即张居正领衔编撰的教科书之一，全书分为上、下两篇，上篇讲述历代帝王励精图治之举，下篇剖析历代帝王倒行逆施之祸。每一则事例都配画一幅，图文并茂地诠释帝王之道。此外，张居正还制作了有大明疆域图与文武官员职名的"职官书屏"，并让吏部每十日更新官员人事变动的情况，用来教导神宗朝政上的运作。

Zhang Juzheng was not only the Senior Grand Secretary, but also oversaw the education of Wanli Emperor. He appointed teachers and readers-in-waiting for the young emperor, personally compiled textbooks for him and taught him classics and history. *Illustrated Textbook for Wanli Emperor* is one of the textbooks compiled mainly by Zhang Juzheng. The book is divided into two parts. Part One talks about the efforts of previous emperors in making the nation strong and prosperous; Part Two analyzes the disasters caused by the wrongdoings of the emperors in the past. Each story is illustrated to interpret the way of governing for state rulers. In addition, Zhang Juzheng also created a "book screen for officials" with a map of the Ming Dynasty's territory and the titles of civil and military officials, and had the Ministry of Personnel update the personnel changes of officials every ten days to teach Emperor Shenzong how the court worked.

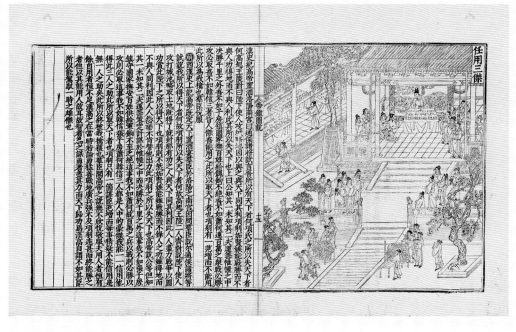

《帝鉴图说》

（明）张居正等编撰 明万历元年（1573 年）潘允端刻本

Illustrated Textbook for Wanli Emperor (Di Jian Tu Shuo)
Compiled by Zhang Juzheng and others, block-printed edition of Pan Yunduan in the 1st year of the Wanli reign of Ming Dynasty (1573)

明代朝廷如何运转？
How did the Ming Court Work?

9

若无疏漏或意见，发至各部执行

Issuing to various ministries to implement if approved and with no careless omissions or opinions.

7

交由司礼监，司礼监根据结果进行批红

Handing them over to the Directorate of Ceremonial, who writes remarks in vermillion ink.

6

各司呈报到部，部门给出明确的结果

Submitting to various ministries where definite results are given.

司礼监
Directorate of Ceremonial
（批红权）
(Right to write imperial rescript in vermillion ink)

六部
Six Ministries
（执行权）
(Right to execute)

皇帝
Emperor

内阁
Grand Secretariat
（票拟权）
(Right to draft remarks)

通政使司、六科
Office of Transmission and Six Offices
（审核权）
(Right to review and revise)

3

皇帝看完后交由内阁

Handing them over to the Grand Secretariat after the emperor finished reading.

2

通政使司传达至皇帝

The Office of Transmission transmitting them to the Emperor

1

内外奏章报至通政使司

Submitting the capital and provincial memorials to the Office of Transmission.

4

内阁票拟给出处理意见

The Grand Secretariat making draft remarks.

5

由相应的各科抄出到司

Forwarding them to the ministries after copying by corresponding Offices.

8

批红后，六科审核

Reviewing and revising by the Six Offices after the emperor or his representatives made the remarks in vermillion ink.

慈圣皇太后李氏像

Portrait of Empress Dowager Cisheng, of the Li clan

Empress Dowager Cisheng, of the Li clan (1545 - 1614) was the biological mother of Wanli Emperor. Although she resided in the deep palace, she was well-versed in practical matters - externally vindicating Zhang Juzheng's authority, supporting him in regulating court affairs; internally and strictly disciplining the young emperor, teaching him to study diligently to become a wise ruler. A pious believer in Buddhism, she built many temples in the capital. In the 5th year of Wanli reign (1577), Empress Dowager Li built the Wanshou Temple (the temple of longevity) west of the Guangyuan Gate outside the Xizhimen to fulfill the wishes of her husband, Emperor Muzong. Many spacious and magnificent buildings were constructed in the temple, such as the Hall of Longevity Extension, the Hall of Arhats, the Hall of Heavenly Kings, the Depositary of Buddhist Texts, the Hall of Skanda, the Hall of Dharma, the Hall of Manjusri, and the Hall of Samantabhadra. It was one of the imperial temples in the Ming Dynasty.

慈圣皇太后李氏（1545～1614年）是万历的生母。李太后虽身居深宫，却深谙事理，对外维护张居正的权威、支持其整饬朝政，对内严厉管教年幼的皇帝，教导其勤学上进、成为一代明君。她笃信佛教，在京城营造了许多寺庙。万历五年（1577年），李太后为完成穆宗遗愿，在西直门外广源闸之西修建万寿寺。寺内有大延寿殿、罗汉殿、天王殿、藏经阁、韦驮殿、达摩殿、文殊殿、普贤殿等建筑，宏敞深静，华焕精严，为明代的皇家寺庙之一。

万寿寺
Wanshou Temple

定兴慈云阁模型

现代
长 66、宽 60、高 70 厘米
中国文化遗产研究院藏

Model of Ciyun Pavilion in Dingxing County

Modern

Length 66 cm, Width 60 cm, Height 70 cm

China Academy of Cultural Heritage

慈云阁原名大悲阁，在河北省保定市定兴县城十字街中心。始建于元代大德十年（1306 年），1996 年被国务院公布为全国第四批重点文物保护单位。慈云阁又名大悲阁，因阁内塑有大悲佛像而得名。明万历年间重加修葺，因佛教礼"心慈为贵，贵慈如云"，故更名为慈云阁。清康熙五十二年（1713 年）、嘉庆二十四年（1819 年）迭次修葺，始具现今规模。

The Ciyun Pavilion, formerly known as the Hall of Great Compassion, is located in the center of Shizi Street, Dingxing County, Baoding City, Hebei Province. It was first built in the 10th year of the Dade reign of Yuan Dynasty (1306), and was declared as the fourth batch of the State Priority Protected Cultural Heritage Sites by the State Council in 1996. The Ciyun Pavilion, or the Hall of Great Compassion, is named after the statue of the Great Compassion Buddha inside the pavilion. It was renovated during the Wanli reign of the Ming Dynasty. As Buddhism valued kindness and compassion, it was renamed the Ciyun Pavilion. It became what it looks like today after the repeated repairs in the 52nd year of the Kangxi reign (1713) and the 24th year of the Jiaqing reign (1819) of the Qing Dynasty.

万历三大征
The Three Great Conquests of Wanli

万历亲操政柄后，一改以往听凭元辅和太后吩咐的形象，强调"事事由朕独断"。年轻的万历励精图治，试图让臣子们刮目相看。他把注意力放在"边事"上，力图重振天朝雄风。万历年间，明朝先后在西北、东北和西南边疆几乎同时开展军事行动，即：宁夏之役、朝鲜之役和播州之役，史称"万历三大征"。"万历三大征"持续近十年，基本以胜利告终，对国家安定和统一而言意义非凡，成为万历在位期间极其辉煌的政绩。

After Wanli Emperor personally took control of the government, his previous image as a "yes-man" to the Senior Grand Secretary and the Empress Dowager also changed. He began to take matters into his own hands. The young emperor strived to make his nation strong and prosperous and to make his courtiers look at him with new eyes. He focused his attention on "border affairs" and tried to revive the majesty of the great empire. During the Wanli reign, the Ming Dynasty successively carried out military operations in the northwest, northeast and southwest borders, namely: The Battle of Ningxia, the Battle of Korea and the Battle of Bozhou, known as the "Three Great Conquests of Wanli" in history, which lasted for nearly ten years and basically ended in victory. They were of great significance for national stability and unity, and became extremely brilliant political achievements of Wanli Emperor during his reign.

明《出警图》局部　台北故宫博物院藏
Painting scroll of *An Imperial Procession* (detail) (Ming)　Collection of Taipei Palace Museum

二 地下玄宫——定陵

万历十一年（1583 年）春，明神宗在天寿山举行春祭礼时，开始为自己卜选陵址。经反复查勘，于次年秋卜定大峪山为寿宫吉地。定陵修建历时六年，于万历十八年完工，耗银 800 万两。万历四十八年七月二十一日，神宗病故于弘德殿，享年五十八岁，十月三日入葬玄宫。定陵在 1956～1957 年进行考古发掘，随葬品多达 3000 余件，涵盖丝织品、帝后冠服、金银器、铜锡器、瓷器、琉璃器、玉石器、漆木器、首饰、仪仗、谥册等，数量众多、品类丰富、制作精良、世所罕见。

In the spring of the 11th year of Wanli reign (1583), while the Emperor Shenzong of Ming held a sacrifice to the god of spring at Tianshou Mountain, he began to select a tomb site for himself. After repeated exploration, in the autumn of the following year, he chose the Dayu Mountain as the auspicious site of his mausoleum. The construction of Dingling Mausoleum took six years and was completed in the 18th year of Wanli reign, consuming 8 million taels of silver. On the 21st day of the seventh month of the 48th year of Wanli reign, Emperor Shenzong died of illness at the Hall of Hongde (Great Virtue) at the age of 58. He was buried in the Underground Palace on the 3rd day of the tenth month. During the archaeological excavations in the Dingling Mausoleum from 1956 to 1957, over 3,000 burial items were discovered, including silk fabrics, imperial crowns and robes, gold and silverware, copper and tinware, porcelain, glassware, jade ware, lacquered wood ware, jewelry, flags and weapons carried by the honor of guards, books of conferring posthumous titles, etc. They were large in quantity, rich in categories, excellent in craftsmanship, the rarely seen in the world.

画卷描绘盛大的皇家谒陵队伍，由北京城德胜门出发，直至皇帝谒陵目的地，离京城四十五公里外的天寿山，这里是明朝历代皇帝的陵寝区。全图以皇帝及其仪卫为主，衬以桃红柳绿，郊野春景之自然景色。

《出警图》中皇帝是唯一一个正面形象，骑黑色高头大马，着金色盔甲，盔甲两臂绣有精美的龙纹，帽子上插着两根白翎，还系着一条红色的缨带，他的脸被画得很大，突出其尊贵的身份。这描绘的可能是明神宗万历皇帝。

The scroll depicts a grand imperial procession setting out from the Deshengmen in Beijing to the destination in the Tianshou Mountain, 45 kilometers away from the capital where the imperial ancestral tombs of the Ming Dynasty are located. The whole painting is themed with the emperor and his honor of guards, setting off with the natural scenery of spring with red peach blossoms and green willows in the outskirts.

The painting presents the front view of an emperor who rides on a big black horse in golden armor. The arms of his armor are embroidered with exquisite dragon designs. His hat is adorned with two upright white feathers and tied with red tassels. His face is painted large, highlighting his noble identity. It could be the image of the Wanli Emperor.

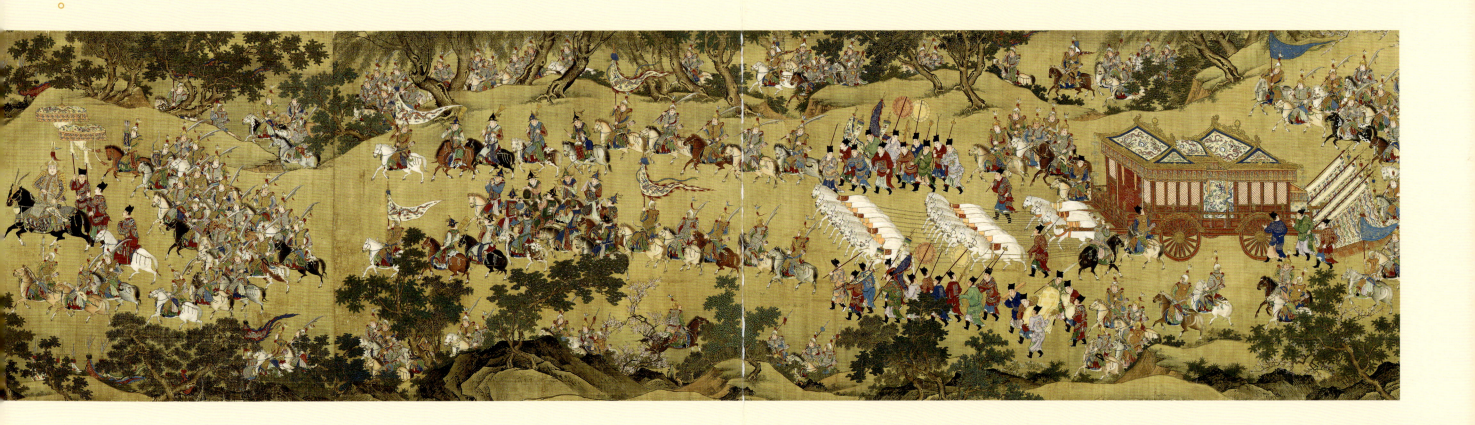

定陵鸟瞰图
Aerial view of the Dingling Mausoleum

明十三陵
The Thirteen Tombs of the Ming Dynasty

明十三陵是明朝帝陵，位于北京市昌平区天寿山南麓，明成祖朱棣在此选定陵址后，改黄土山为天寿山。此后，明朝十六位皇帝中，除太祖朱元璋葬在南京孝陵、第二代皇帝惠宗朱允炆下落不明、第七代皇帝代宗朱祁钰葬在北京西郊玉泉山景泰陵外，其余十三位均葬于天寿山，因此统称"明十三陵"。

明十三陵自永乐七年（1409 年）五月启用，依次建有长陵（成祖）、献陵（仁宗）、景陵（宣宗）、裕陵（英宗）、茂

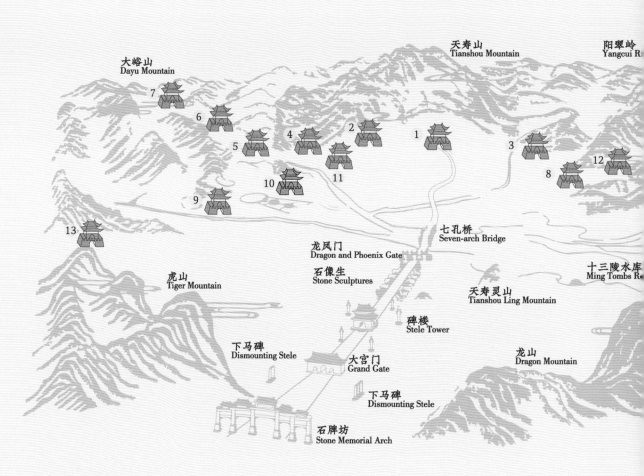

十三陵陵寝位置图
Location of the thirteen mausoleums of the Ming Tombs

陵（宪宗）、泰陵（孝宗）、康陵（武宗）、永陵（世宗）、昭陵（穆宗）、定陵（神宗）、庆陵（光宗）、德陵（熹宗）、思陵（思宗）。这些帝陵以长陵为中心组成庞大的帝陵群，十三陵的每座帝陵都有各自的享殿（祾恩殿）、明楼、宝城，长陵的神道成为一条贯穿各陵的"总神道"。陵区四面群山环抱，景致幽静，以山川大聚之势，构建起帝陵山川形胜的优渥环境，是世界上现存规模最大、帝后陵寝最多的帝陵建筑群，也是全球保存最完整的皇家墓葬群之一。

	长陵	Changling Mausoleum
1	长陵	Changling Mausoleum
2	献陵	Xianling Mausoleum
3	景陵	Jingling Mausoleum
4	裕陵	Yuling Mausoleum
5	茂陵	Maoling Mausoleum
6	泰陵	Tailing Mausoleum
7	康陵	Kangling Mausoleum
8	永陵	Yongling Mausoleum
9	昭陵	Zhaoling Mausoleum
⑩	定陵	Dingling Mausoleum
11	庆陵	Qingling Mausoleum
12	德陵	Deling Mausoleum
13	思陵	Siling Mausoleum

The Ming Thirteen Tombs are the imperial mausoleums of the Ming Dynasty, located at the southern foot of Tianshou Mountain in Changping District, Beijing. The Huangtu Mountain was renamed to Tianshou Mountain after Emperor Chengzu of Ming Zhu Di selected the tomb site here. Among the sixteen emperors of the Ming Dynasty, Emperor Taizu Zhu Yuanzhang was buried at Xiaoling Mausoleum in Nanjing. The burial place of the 2nd Emperor Huizong Zhu Yunwen was unknown. The 7th Emperor Daizong Zhu Qiyu was buried at Jingtai Mausoleum in Yuquan Mountain, western suburbs of Beijing. All the other thirteen emperors were buried at the Tianshou Mountain, hence collectively known as the "Thirteen Tombs of the Ming Dynasty".

The Ming Thirteen Tombs were put into use in the fifth month of the 17th year of Yongle reign (1409), and were successively built with Changling (Chengzu), Xianling (Renzong), Jingling (Xuanzong), Yuling (Yingzong), Maoling (Xianzong), Tailing (Xiaozong), Kangling (Wuzong), Yongling (Shizong), Zhaoling (Muzong), Dingling (Shenzong), Qingling (Guangzong), Deling (Xizong), and Siling (Sizong) mausoleums. These imperial mausoleums form a large complex of imperial mausoleums centered on the Changling Mausoleum. Each imperial mausoleum of the Ming Tombs has its own Sacrifice-Offering Palace (Sacrificial Hall), Soul Tower, and Rampart. The spirit road of the Changling Mausoleum has become a "general spirit road" running through all the mausoleums. The cemetery is surrounded by mountains on all sides, with a serene scenery. With the momentum of the gathering of mountains and rivers, it creates a picturesque environment for the imperial tombs. The Ming Tombs are the largest existing imperial tomb complex in the world with the largest number of tombs of emperors and empresses, and also one of the most completely preserved royal tombs in the world.

定陵建筑格局

Architectural Structure of the Dingling Mausoleum

定陵的规模、形制仿明世宗永陵而建，"规制尽美，福祚无疆"。主要建筑有祾恩门、祾恩殿、明楼、宝城和地下宫殿，占地18.2万平方米。明楼的檐枋、斗拱全部用预制石件构成，再髹漆施彩；宝城垛口、明楼地面等处均用花斑石铺砌；宝城外筑一圈外罗城。定陵玄宫全部为石结构。所用砖一种是铺地方砖，烧自苏州，质地极其细腻，如沙中澄金，俗称金砖；另一种是白城砖，绝大部分产自山东临清。

定陵建筑是仿照帝王生前所居住的皇宫建筑的格局修建的，地面建筑相当于皇宫的外朝部分，而玄宫建筑则相当于皇宫的内廷的"九重法宫"格局。定陵地面建筑中的祾恩殿、明楼、宝顶相当于皇宫中奉天、华盖、谨身三大殿的位置，祾恩殿两侧的配殿相当于文华、武英二殿的位置，祾恩门的位置又相当于奉天门。定陵玄宫前面有砖隧道、石隧道和封门的金刚墙，玄宫的前、中、后三殿室。

The scale shape and structure of the Dingling Mausoleum are modeled after the Yongling Mausoleum of Emperor Shizong of Ming, with "perfect structure and boundless blessings". The main buildings include the Sacrificial Gate, the Sacrificial Hall, the Soul Tower, Ramparts, and underground palaces, covering an area of 182,000 square meters. The eave purlins and arches of the Soul Tower are all made of prefabricated stone pieces, and then painted with lacquer; The battlements of ramparts and the ground of Soul Tower are paved with mottled stones; a ring of outer wall is built outside the ramparts. The underground palaces of the Dingling Mausoleum are all masonry structures. One type of brick used is the square brick for paving, fired in Suzhou, with extremely fine texture, looking like gold in sand, commonly known as golden brick; The other type is the white city wall brick, mainly produced in Linqing, Shandong.

The architectural structure of Dingling Mausoleum was built after that of the imperial palace where the emperor lived during his lifetime. The surface structures are equivalent to the outer court of the imperial palace, while the underground structures are equivalent to the "Nine-Square Grid Architectural Structure" of the inner court of the imperial palace. The positions of the surface structures of the Sacrificial Hall, the Soul Tower, and Rampart in the Dingling Mausoleum are equivalent to those of the three main halls of the Hall of Great Harmony, the Hall of Splendid Canopy, and the Hall of Practicing Moral Culture in the imperial palace. The positions of the side chamber on either side of the Sacrificial are equivalent to those of the Hall of Literary Glory and the Hall of Military Prowess, and the position of the gate of the Sacrificial Hall is equivalent to that of the Fengtian Gate. There are brick passages, stone passages, and closed-door parapets as well as the front, central, and rear chambers in front of the Underground Palace in Dingling Mausoleum.

a. 宝顶　Rampart
b. 明楼　Soul Tower
c. 祾恩殿　Sacrificial Hall
d. 左庑　Left corridor
e. 右庑　Right corridor

A. 谨身殿（建极殿）　Hall of Practicing Moral Culture (Jianji Hall)
B. 华盖殿（中极殿）　Hall of Splendid Canopy (Zhongji Hall)
C. 奉天殿（皇极殿）　Hall of Great Harmony（Huangji Hall）
D. 文华殿　Hall of Literary
E. 武英殿　Hall of Military Prowess

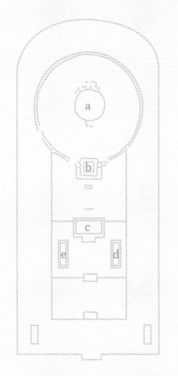

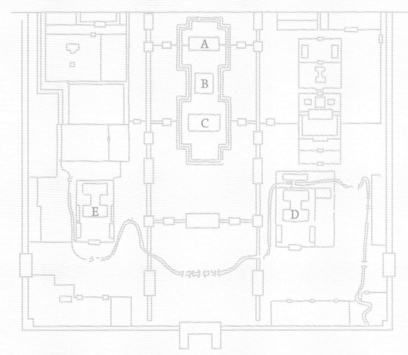

明定陵地面建筑与明代皇宫外朝建筑比较图

Comparison between the surface structures of the Ming Dingling Mausoleum and the Outer Court structures of the Ming Imperial Palace

九重法宫

The Nine-Square Grid Architectural Structure

定陵地宫体现了明代九重法宫，即明代皇宫内廷建筑格局的特点。所谓"九重法宫"之制，是指我国古代帝王居住和祭祀的宫殿规制，古人认为它以纵横各三，形成棋盘型的九宫平面图。在九宫当中，中央一宫称太室，中上称玄堂，中下称明堂，中左称总章，中右称青阳，四角四殿称作个室。

The Dingling Underground Palace embodies the characteristics of the Nine-Square Grid Architectural Structure, namely the architectural structure of the inner court of the imperial palace of the Ming Dynasty. The so-called "The Nine-Square Grid Architectural Structure" system refers to the regulations of the emperor's palaces for residence and worship in ancient China. The ancients believed that it formed a chessboard-shaped plan of nine grids with three vertical and three horizontal sections. Among the nine palaces, the central one is known as *Taishi*, the central hall; the upper middle is known as *Xuantang*, the northern hall; the lower middle is called *Mingtang*, the southern hall; the middle left is known as *Zongzhang*, the western hall; the middle right is known as *Qingyang*, the eastern hall; the four halls at the corners are known as individual chambers.

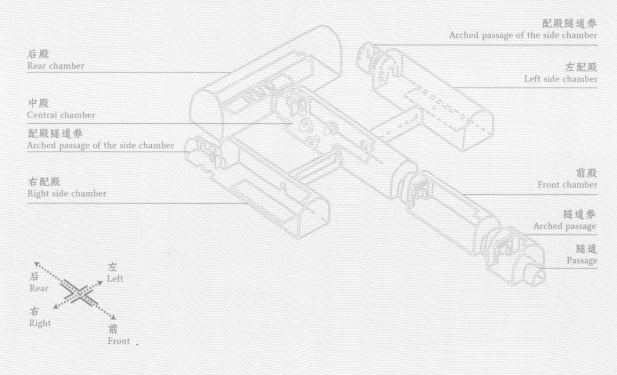

后殿
Rear chamber

中殿
Central chamber

配殿隧道券
Arched passage of the side chamber

右配殿
Right side chamber

配殿隧道券
Arched passage of the side chamber

左配殿
Left side chamber

前殿
Front chamber

隧道券
Arched passage

隧道
Passage

后
Rear

左
Left

右
Right

前
Front

定陵玄宫透视图
Perspective view of the Underground Palace of Dingling Mausoleum

前殿是玄宫前部第一座石门内的殿室，无任何陈设，有石门一座与中室相通，客观上只起到一个穿堂的作用。

中殿前后有石门可与前后殿室相通，左右有甬道和石门与左右两侧室相通，是通往前、后、左、右四殿室的中枢殿室。殿内陈设有一帝二后的汉白玉神座，座前各有一套黄色琉璃五供（香炉一、烛台二、花瓶二），以及一盏由青花云龙纹瓷缸储油、内置油瓢和灯捻的长明灯。陈设象征着帝后的神灵在阴间的"九重法宫"之内，同样要日理万机、秉执宫壸（kǔn）之仪。

后殿是玄宫的主室，又有"玄堂""皇堂"之称，是安奉帝后梓宫和随葬物品的地方。后殿居中部位是宝座（棺床），宝座正中留有方形孔穴，内填黄土，称为"金井"。宝座上分别置帝后棺椁，万历帝居中，孝端后居左，孝靖后居右。棺椁周围放置有玉料、梅瓶及装满殉葬品的二十六只红漆木箱。

The front chamber is the chamber inside the first stone gate in the front of the Underground Palace, without any furnishings. The stone gate is connected to the central chamber, only serving as a hallway objectively.

There are stone gates in the front and rear of the central chamber to connect with the front and rear chambers, and there are corridors and stone gates on the left and right that connect with the left and right chambers, serving as the central chamber that leads to the front, rear, left, and right chambers. The chamber is furnished with three white marble thrones respective to the emperor and his two empresses. A set of five yellow glazed sacrificial vessels (1 incense burner, 2 candlesticks, 2 vases), and an ever-burning lamp - with a blue-and-white porcelain jar with the design of dragons and clouds for storing oil, an oil ladle and a lamp wick. The furnishings symbolize that the spirits of the emperor and empresses attend to numerous affairs every day and observe the ethical norms even in the underworld.

The rear chamber is the main room of the Underground Palace, also known as the "Xuantang" and "Huangtang". It is where the coffins of the emperor and his empresses and their burial objects enshrined. The central part of the rear chamber is the coffin platform, with a square hole left in the center and filled with loess, known as the coffin pit. Three coffins are placed on the platform, with Wanli Emperor's in the center, Empress Xiaoduan's on the left, and Empress Xiaojing's on the right. There are jade materials, prunus vases, and 26 red lacquered wooden boxes filled with sacrificial items placed around the coffins.

玄宫中殿原状
The original state of the central chamber of the Underground Palace

玄宫后殿原状
The original state of the rear chamber of the Underground Palace

明神宗皇帝像
台北故宫博物院藏
Portrait of Emperor Shenzong of the Ming Dynasty
Collection of Taipei Palace Museum

明神宗朱翊钧（1563～1620年），明朝第十三位皇帝，明穆宗朱载垕（jì）第三子。生于嘉靖四十二年（1563年）八月十七日，隆庆二年（1568年）三月十一日立为皇太子，隆庆六年（1572年）六月十日即位，次年改元万历。万历四十八年（1620年）七月二十一日驾崩，享年58岁，九月上尊谥为"范天合道哲肃敦简光文章武安仁止孝显皇帝"，庙号神宗，十月三日葬明定陵。明神宗在位48年，为明朝在位时间最长的皇帝。

The Emperor Shenzong of Ming Zhu Yijun (1563 - 1620), the thirteenth emperor of the Ming Dynasty and the third son of the Emperor Muzong of Ming Zhu Zaiji, born on the 17th day of the eighth month of the 42nd year of Jiajing reign (1563), was conferred the Crown Prince on the 11th day of the third month of the 2nd year of Longqing reign (1568). He ascended to the throne on the 10th of the sixth month of the 6th year of the Longqing reign (1572), and a year later, changed his reign title to the first year of Wanli reign. He died on the 21st day of the seventh month of the 48th year of Wanli reign (1620), at the age of 58. In the ninth month, he was posthumously honored with the title of "Emperor Fantian Hedao Zhesu Dunjian Guangwen Zhangwu Anren Zhixiao Xian", with the temple name Shenzong. He was buried in the Dingling Mausoleum of the Ming Tombs on the 3rd day of the tenth month. The Emperor Shenzong of Ming reigned for 48 years and was the longest-reigning emperor of the Ming Dynasty.

孝端皇后王氏（1564～1620年），浙江余姚人，永年伯王伟之女。生于京师，万历六年（1578年）二月册立为皇后。《明史·后妃传》称其"性端谨""正位中宫者四十二年，以慈孝称"。万历四十八年（1620年）四月病故，上尊谥为"孝端贞恪庄惠仁明媲天毓圣显皇后"，十月三日葬于明定陵。

Empress Xiaoduan, of the Wang clan (1564 - 1620), born in Yuyao, Zhejiang, was the daughter of Yongnian Earl Wang Wei. She was born in the capital, and was conferred the empress in the second month of the 6th year of Wanli reign (1578). *History of Ming: Biographies of Empresses and Consorts* said that she was "graceful and discreet in nature" and "mastered the harem as empress for 42 years, and was known for her compassion and filial piety." She died of illness in the fourth month of the 48th year of Wanli reign (1620) and was posthumously honored with the title of "Empress Xiaoduan Zhenke Zhuanghui Renming Pitian Yusheng Xian", and was buried in the Dingling Mausoleum of the Ming Tombs on the 3rd day of the tenth month.

孝端皇后像
台北故宫博物院藏
Portrait of Empress Xiaoduan
Collection of Taipei Palace Museum

孝靖皇后王氏（1565～1611年），明光宗朱常洛生母，宣府都司左卫人，原任锦衣卫百户赠明威将军指挥佥事王朝寀（cǎi）之女。生于嘉靖四十四年（1565年），万历六年（1578年）选入皇宫。初为慈宁宫宫人，侍奉孝定皇太后，万历十年（1582年）六月册封为恭妃，同年八月生光宗朱常洛。万历三十四年四月晋封为皇贵妃，万历三十九年（1611年）九月病故。明熹宗朱由校即位后，为其上尊谥为"孝靖温懿敬让贞慈参天胤圣皇太后"，迁葬明定陵。

Empress Xiaojing, of the Wang clan (1565 - 1611), the biological mother of the Emperor Guangzong of Ming Zhu Changluo, a native of Zuowei of Xuanfu Prefecture, and daughter of Wang Chaocai, was born in the 44th year of the Jiajing reign (1565), and was elected into the palace in the 6th year of Wanli reign (1578). She was originally an attendant in the Palace of Compassion and Tranquility serving the Empress Dowager Xiaoding and was conferred the title of Consort Gong in the sixth month of the 10th year of Wanlin reign (1582). In the eighth month of the same year, she gave birth to Zhu Changluo. She was promoted to the title of Imperial Noble Consort in the fourth month of the 34th year of Wanli, and died of illness in the ninth month of the 39th year of Wanli reign. After the Emperor Xizong of Ming Zhu Youjiao ascended to the throne, he posthumously honored her with the title of "Empress Dowager Xiaojing Wenyi Jingrang Zhenci Yinsheng", and moved her graveyard to the Ding Mausoleum of the Ming Tombs.

孝靖皇后像
台北故宫博物院藏
Portrait of Empress Xiaojing
Collection of Taipei Palace Museum

孝端皇后谥宝

明万历
北京市昌平区明十三陵定陵出土
通高 13.4、边长 12.4~13 厘米
明十三陵博物馆藏

Burial seal incised with the posthumous title of Empress Xiaoduan

Wanli reign of Ming Dynasty

Unearthed from the Dingling Mausoleum of the Ming Tombs in Changping District, Beijing

Overall Height 13.4 cm, Length of Side 12.4 - 13 cm

The Ming Tombs Museum

谥宝是古代帝后陵墓中刻有谥号的玺印，表示墓主的身份、称号和地位，有石、玉、木等材质。

此件孝端皇后谥宝，印文为阳文篆书"孝端贞恪庄惠仁明媲天毓圣显皇后宝"四行十六字。孝端皇后去世后，神宗于万历四十八年七月十三日为其上尊谥"孝端皇后"。同年九月十三日，其孙熹宗朱由校为其上尊谥为"孝端贞恪庄惠仁明媲天毓圣显皇后"。这件谥宝是熹宗为孝端皇后制作并陪葬的。

Burial seal is a seal of the ancient emperor or empress made of stone, jade, wood, or other materials incised with his or her posthumous title buried in the tomb, indicating the identity, title, and status of the tomb's owner.

This seal is incised with 16 characters of "Seal of Emperess Xiaoduan Zhenke Zhuanghui Renming Pitian Yusheng Xian" in four lines. After the death of Empress Xiaoduan, Emperor Shenzong honored her with the posthumous title of "Empress Xiaoduan" on the 13th day of the seventh month of the 48th year of Wanli. On the 13th day of the ninth month of the same year, her grandson Emperor Xizong Zhu Youjiao honored her with the title of "Emperess Xiaoduan Zhenke Zhuanghui Renming Pitian Yusheng Xian" and made the seal to be buried along her side.

玉料

明万历
北京市昌平区明十三陵定陵出土
长 53、宽 22、厚 20.5 厘米
明十三陵博物馆藏

Jade material

Wanli reign of Ming Dynasty

Unearthed from the Dingling Mausoleum of the Ming Tombs
in Changping District, Beijing

Length 53 cm, Width 22 cm, Thickness 20.5 cm

The Ming Tombs Museum

定陵地宫内棺椁周围放置有玉料、梅瓶及装满陪葬品的红漆木箱。此玉料为随葬玉料之一。每具棺椁南北两侧各放玉料四块，东端一块，孝端皇后的梓宫内又增放四块。玉料的大小形态不一，大部分有墨书文字，记录玉料的名称和重量。据《汉书·杨王孙传》称"口含玉石，欲化不得，郁为枯腊"。为保尸身不腐，中国古代帝王多有玉料殉葬。

Jade materials, prunus vases, and red lacquered wooden boxes filled with burial items were placed around the coffins in the underground palace of Dingling Mausoleum. This jade material is one of the burial jade materials. Four pieces of jade materials were placed on the south and north sides of each coffin, one on the east end. Four more pieces were placed in the coffin of Empress Xiaoduan. The size and shape of jade materials vary, and most of them have ink scripts recording the name and weight of the jade material. There is a saying in *Book of Han: Biography of Yang Wangsun*, "With jade held in mouth, the body will turn into a dry body in days and will not transform". To prevent the corpses from decay, the jade materials were buried in the imperial tombs in ancient China.

黄琉璃釉陶蜡台 （2 件）

明万历
北京市昌平区明十三陵定陵出土
通高 22.5~22.8、盘径 26~26.5、圈足径 24~25 厘米
明十三陵博物馆藏

Yellow glazed pottery candlestick (2 pcs)

Wanli reign of Ming Dynasty

Unearthed from the Dingling Mausoleum of the Ming Tombs
in Changping District, Beijing

Overall Height 22.5 - 22.8 cm, Diameter of Disc
26 - 26.5 cm, Diameter of Ring Foot 24 - 25 cm

The Ming Tombs Museum

定陵玄宫中殿内帝、后每一神座前，中间置香炉一件，左右各置烛台一座、花瓶一只，均置于束腰型汉白玉石座上，即所谓的"五供"。这批琉璃器，均呈深黄色，胎质较粗，含有沙粒，火候高，施釉较厚，且个别地方厚薄不匀，表面有开片纹，类似瓷器。

They were placed before the thrones of the emperor and his empresses in the central chamber of the underground palace at the time of excavation. In front of each throne, an incense burner was placed in the middle, with a candlestick and a vase placed on its left and right. All of these were placed on the narrow-waist-shaped white marble stone pedestal, commonly known as the "five sacrificial vessels". This group of glazed items is dark yellow, with coarse body texture, containing grains of sand, fired with high temperature, thickly and unevenly glazed, with cracks on the surface, more like porcelain.

黄琉璃釉陶花瓶 (2件)

明万历

北京市昌平区明十三陵定陵出土

通高 35、口径 10.5、圈足径 16.5 厘米

明十三陵博物馆藏

Yellow glazed pottery vase (2 pcs)

Wanli reign of Ming Dynasty

Unearthed from the Dingling Mausoleum of the Ming Tombs in Changping District, Beijing

Overall Height 35 cm, Mouth Diameter 10.5 cm, Diameter of Ring Foot 16.5 cm

The Ming Tombs Museum

子母口，细颈，圆鼓腹，喇叭形圈足，颈两侧附有衔环铺首，环贴于腹上。盖为扁圆形，下有子口，其上有六个插孔，孔上下不通，似乎是为随葬而做的明器。

Covered mouth, thin neck, round drum-shaped belly, trumpet-shaped ring foot, with looped knocker ears on either side of the neck, and the loops attached to the belly. The cover is oblate with a sub-mouth underneath and six sockets on top, seemed to be the burial objects made for the dead.

青花云龙纹缸

明嘉靖
北京市昌平区明十三陵定陵出土
通高 70、口径 71.1、底径 58.5 厘米
明十三陵博物馆藏

Blue-and-white porcelain vat with the cloud and dragon design

Jiajing reign of Ming Dynasty
Unearthed from the Dingling Mausoleum of the Ming Tombs in Changping District, Beijing
Overall Height 70 cm, Mouth Diameter 71.1 cm, Bottom Diameter 58.5 cm
The Ming Tombs Museum

定陵共出土 3 件青花云龙纹缸，玄宫中殿帝、后神座前各一件，位于"五供"之前。出土时缸内贮有油脂，表层为蜂蜡，已经凝固，下部为芝麻香油。油面有铜制圆瓢子一个，中心有灯芯，芯端有燃烧的痕迹，大概是安葬时点燃的，玄宫封闭后，氧气耗尽熄灭。这便是所谓的"长明灯"或"万年灯"。此为孝端皇后神座前长明灯。

此缸外部有"大明嘉靖年制"题款，口部饰卷草纹一周，颈部及近底部各饰莲瓣纹一周，腹部绘云龙纹，云飘逸流动，龙矫健有力；两龙一前一后昂首曲颈，腾跃于流云之中，栩栩如生，充满神韵。

明代瓷器在中国瓷器发展史上最负盛名，尤以白地蓝花的青花瓷为精。景德镇是明代的制瓷中心，专设御窑厂为宫廷生产瓷器。文献记载，这种巨型龙缸烧造极为困难，每窑每年烧制不足三只，且专供皇室。为满足宫廷需要，在御窑厂专设龙缸窑 32 座，专门掌握烧造龙缸技术的工匠称"龙缸匠"。青花瓷是明代景德镇生产瓷器的主流，至正德、嘉靖时期，青花瓷的烧制已达到炉火纯青的境界。嘉靖之后，产自南洋的釉料"苏麻离青"渐已绝迹，青花瓷的烧制不如从前，这也是为何万历皇帝的定陵随葬的青花云龙纹缸为嘉靖年间所制。

A total of three blue-and-white porcelain vats with the dragon and cloud design were unearthed from Dingling Mausoleum, with each placed in front of the thrones of the emperor and his two empresses respectively in the central chamber of the underground palace, before the "five sacrificial vessels". There was sesame oil stored in the vats at the time of excavation, with a layer of solidified beeswax on the surface. There was a copper round ladle on the oil surface, with a wick in the center and burned traces at the wick tip, which could have been ignited at the time of burial. After the Underground Palace was sealed, it died out due to lacking oxygen. This is the so-called "ever-burning lamp". This piece is the ever-burning lamp in front of the throne of Empress Xiaoduan.

The vat is inscribed with "Made in the Jiajing reign of the Great Ming dynasty" on the outer wall. The mouth is decorated with a ring of floral scroll design, the neck and near the bottom of each decorated with a ring of lotus petal design. The belly is painted with cloud and dragon design, with clouds floating freely and the dragons powerful and agile; the two dragons, one in front and one on the back, soar amidst the flowing clouds with curved necks, very lifelike and fascinating.

Ming Dynasty porcelain enjoys a great reputation in the development history of Chinese porcelain, remarkably the blue-and-white porcelain. Jingdezhen was a center of porcelain production during the Ming Dynasty, specializing in the imperial kiln to produce porcelain for the court. According to literature records, it was extremely difficult to fire such colossal dragon vats. Each kiln produced no more than three pieces per year and these were dedicated to the imperial household. In order to meet the needs of the court, 32 dragon vat kilns were set up in the imperial kiln. The technicians who specialized in firing dragon vats were called "dragon vat artisans". Blue-and-white porcelain was the mainstream of Jingdezhen's porcelain production during the Ming Dynasty. By the Zhengde and Jiajing reigns, the firing of blue-and-white porcelain had reached the peak of perfection. After the Jiajing reign, the glaze material "Suma Liqing" produced in the Nanyang region gradually disappeared, and the firing of blue-and-white porcelain decreased. This was also why the blue-and-white porcelain vats with the cloud and dragon design buried in the Dingling Mausoleum of Wanli Emperor were made during the Jiajing reign.

素三彩蟠螭纹三足炉

明万历
北京市昌平区明十三陵定陵出土
通高 17.6、口径 15.8 厘米
明十三陵博物馆藏

Susancai (plain tricolor) three-legged incense burner with coiling-*Chi* designs

Wanli reign of Ming Dynasty
Unearthed from the Dingling Mausoleum of the Ming Tombs in Changping District, Beijing
Overall Height 17.6 cm, Mouth Diameter 15.8 cm
The Ming Tombs Museum

出于万历帝椁北侧。黄釉地，饰紫、绿、蓝三色。三足由三螭首构成，作仰视透雕式，二螭尾上卷形成两个炉耳，饰透雕灵芝花纹。一螭尾部贴于炉腹形成半浮雕式花纹。炉底外壁有款文两行："大明万历年制"。

整件炉体设计新颖，造型别致，蟠螭屈曲盘绕，流畅自然。炉内还有三齿形铜香靠一件，上宽下窄，齿顶端呈箭鳞形，下端为尖状，三齿之间连二横带，上部一带中间附一圆鼻，相接部分均用铆钉铆合。

It was unearthed on the north side of Wanli Emperor's coffin. Yellow glazed surface, decorated with purple, green, and blue. The three legs are made into three up-looking heads of *Chi* (a dragon whose horns have not grown) in openwork. Two tails are coiled up to form the burner's loop handles, decorated with glossy ganoderma designs in openwork. The tail of a *Chi* is attached to the burner's belly to form a semi-relief pattern. There are two lines of inscriptions on the outer wall of the bottom: "Made in the Wanli reign of the Great Ming dynasty".

The entire burner is novel in design and unique in shape, looking smooth and natural with coiling *Chi*. A three-tooth copper piece is set in the burner for joss sticks to lean on, with a wide top and narrow bottom. The top of the teeth is in the shape of an arrow scale, and the bottom is pointed. Two crossbands connect the three teeth, with a round nose attached in the middle of the upper band. The connecting parts are all riveted together.

明器

Funerary Objects

中国自古便有"事死如事生"的观念。至高无上的万历皇帝，更是早早为自己安排好了身后事。定陵的陵寝建造豪华，陪葬丰厚，让我们看到了生前富贵、死后享乐的始终如一。

定陵出土的陪葬品中，除了帝后生前使用的器物，也有专门制作、仅用于殉葬的明器。明器基本没有实用价值，制作粗疏，仅具其形。明代帝陵沿用随葬明器这一古礼，器物质地多为锡、铜、陶、木，包括卤簿、生活用具、俑等。

It has been a traditional notion in China to serve the dead as they lived. The Wanli Emperor had already arranged matters for his afterlife. The Dingling Mausoleum was extravagantly built and was lavishly stuffed with burial objects, showcasing the consistency of wealth and pleasure during life and after death.

Among the burial objects unearthed from the Dingling Mausoleum, in addition to the objects used by the emperor and empress during their lifetime, there are also funerary objects specifically made to bury the dead. The funerary objects have little practical value, and were roughly made for their forms. The Ming Dynasty imperial tombs followed the ancient rituals of burying the funerary objects, including *Lubu*, daily utensils and figurines and so on, which were mostly made of tin, copper, pottery and wood.

定陵随葬箱内铜锡明器放置情况

The arrangement condition of the copper and tin funerary objects in the burial box of Dingling Mausoleum

铜香炉

明万历
北京市昌平区明十三陵定陵出土
炉高 10.3、口径 7.5、圈足径 8、链长 24.6 厘米
明十三陵博物馆藏

Copper incense burner

Wanli reign of Ming Dynasty

Unearthed from the Dingling Mausoleum of the Ming Tombs
in Changping District, Beijing

Burner: Height 10.3 cm, Mouth Diameter 7.5 cm, Diameter
of Ring Foot 8 cm; Length of Chain 24.6 cm

The Ming Tombs Museum

据《大明会典·大丧礼》记载，帝、后死后随葬明器"照依生存所用卤簿器物名件"。又《大明会典》卷一百八十二《大驾卤簿》及一百八十三《皇后卤簿》中均载："金交椅一把，金脚踏一个，金水盆一个，金水罐一个，金香炉一个，金唾盂一个，金唾壶一个……"出自定陵第七箱内的铜明器有水罐、水盆、香盒、香炉、唾盂、唾壶、交椅、脚踏等各两件，除脚踏缺标签外，每件器物均贴有墨书纸标签标明器物名称和数量。

According to the *Collected Statutes of the Ming Dynasty: The Imperial Mourning Rites*, the funerary objects for the deceased emperors and empresses "should refer to *Lubu* objects they used when they were alive." It is accounted in Volume 182 *Dajia Lubu* and Volume 183 Empress *Lubu* of *Collected Statutes of the Ming Dynasty*: "A gold folding chair, a gold footstool, a gold basin, a gold water pot, a gold incense burner, a gold cuspidor, a gold spittoon pot..." The copper funerary objects unearthed in Box 7 of the Dingling Mausoleum include two jars, two basins, two powder boxes, two censers, two spittoons, two cuspidors, two folding chairs, and two footstools, etc. Except the footstools, each object is tagged with a paper label in ink scripts indicating the name and quantity of the objects.

铜交椅

明万历

北京市昌平区明十三陵定陵出土

通高 15.2、上宽 14.7、底宽 13.8 厘米

明十三陵博物馆藏

Copper folding chair

Wanli reign of Ming Dynasty

Unearthed from the Dingling Mausoleum of the Ming Tombs in Changping District, Beijing

Overall Height 15.2 cm, Width of Top 14.7 cm, Width of Bottom 13.8 cm

The Ming Tombs Museum

这件铜交椅是定陵随葬明器之一，是仿照帝后生前仪仗用器制作的，并没有实用价值。交椅原本是古时一种能折叠的椅子，因椅足交叉而得名，由于搬运方便，常为郊游、围猎、行军作战所用，后逐渐演变成厅堂家具。定陵中共出土两件铜交椅，应是分别为孝端后、孝靖后随葬所用。

The copper folding chair is one of the funerary objects in the Dingling Mausoleum, modeled after the ceremonial vessels used by emperors and empresses during their lifetime, and has no practical use in terms of its function. The chair was originally a folding chair in ancient times, named after its crossed legs. As it was easy to carry, often used for outings, hunting, and military operations. Later, it gradually evolved as household furniture. Two copper folding chairs were unearthed from the Dingling Mausoleum and should be the burial objects of Empress Xiaoduan and Empress Xiaojing, respectively.

锡香匙箸瓶

明万历
北京市昌平区明十三陵定陵出土
高 14.84、口径 6.47、底径 6.8 厘米
明十三陵博物馆藏

Tin bottle for holding incense spoon and chopsticks

Wanli reign of Ming Dynasty

Unearthed from the Dingling Mausoleum of the Ming Tombs in Changping District, Beijing

Height 14.84 cm, Mouth Diameter 6.47 cm, Bottom Diameter 6.8 cm

The Ming Tombs Museum

瓶口焊有象征性的一匙二箸。腹部贴有标签，墨书"锡香匙箸瓶"。

The mouth of the bottle is welded with a symbolic spoon and two chopsticks. The belly is tagged with the ink scripts: "Tin bottle for holding incense spoon and chopsticks".

锡汁瓶

明万历
北京市昌平区明十三陵定陵出土
通高 11.5、口径 2.8、底径 3.1 厘米
明十三陵博物馆藏

Tin gravy bottle

Wanli reign of Ming Dynasty

Unearthed from the Dingling Mausoleum of the Ming Tombs
in Changping District, Beijing

Overall Height 11.5 cm, Mouth Diameter 2.8 cm,
Bottom Diameter 3.1 cm

The Ming Tombs Museum

一侧有耳形把，另一侧有用锡片剪制成的象征性
流。颈部贴有标签，墨书"锡汁瓶"。

It has an ear-shaped handle on one side and a symbolic spout made
of a cut tin slice on the other side. A label is attached to the neck
written with "tin gravy holder" in ink.

锡酒瓮

明万历
北京市昌平区明十三陵定陵出土
高 13.43、口径 6.95、底径 6.75 厘米
明十三陵博物馆藏

Tin wine jar

Wanli reign of Ming Dynasty

Unearthed from the Dingling Mausoleum of the Ming Tombs
in Changping District, Beijing

Height 13.43 cm, Mouth Diameter 6.95 cm,
Bottom Diameter 6.75 cm

The Ming Tombs Museum

肩、腹部焊接有用锡片剪制成的象征性酒勺，腹部贴有标签，墨书"锡酒瓮"。

A symbolic wine scoop cut of tin slices is welded to the shoulder and belly of the jar. A label is attached to the belly written with "tin wine jar" in ink.

锡果碟

明万历
北京市昌平区明十三陵定陵出土
高 0.8、直径 6.43、底径 4.9 厘米
明十三陵博物馆藏

Tin fruit dish

Wanli reign of Ming Dynasty
Unearthed from the Dingling Mausoleum of the Ming Tombs
in Changping District, Beijing
Height 0.8 cm, Diameter 6.43 cm, Bottom Diameter 4.9 cm
The Ming Tombs Museum

定陵这批锡明器均为打制、焊接而成。素面。一般器型较小制作较为粗糙。根据器物的不同形状，首先剪制锡片，分别打制成口、颈、腹、底、盖以及耳、把、环、钮和提梁等，然后焊接成形。所有器物的器盖均与器身焊接在一起。一些器物的附件如耳、把、提梁、盖钮以及酒缸、酒瓮上的酒勺等则用锡片剪制成象征性的部件，不加任何修整，焊接上去。关于它们的用途，一部分器物是作为仪仗明器随葬，而另一部分则为象征性的日常生活用具。

This batch of tin funerary objects was forged and welded in plain face. Most of them were small in size and made in a rough way. Based on the different shapes of the objects, first cut the tin sheets and forged into mouths, necks, bellies, bottoms, covers as well as ears, handles, rings, knobs, and loop handles and then welded into shapes. All the objects had their covers and bodies soldered together. The fittings of some objects, such as ears, handles, loop handles, knobs, as well as wine spoons on wine vats and wine jars were cut into symbolic tin sheets and soldered on without any trimming or polishing. These burial objects were either used for ceremonial purposes or symbolic daily necessities.

正面
The Front

背面
The Back

正面
The Front

背面
The Back

金"吉祥如意"钱（2枚）

明万历
北京市昌平区明十三陵定陵出土
直径 7.3 厘米
明十三陵博物馆藏

Gilded coins carved with "*Jixiang Ruyi* (good luck and best wishes)" (2 pcs)

Wanli reign of Ming Dynasty

Unearthed from the Dingling Mausoleum of the Ming Tombs in Changping District, Beijing

Diameter 7.3 cm

The Ming Tombs Museum

出自万历帝的夹褥上。正面錾阳文"吉祥如意"四字，背面朱书藏文咒语，意为人神相通，消灾祛病。

They were found on the bed sheets of Wanli Emperor. The observe is engraved with four characters of "*Jixiang Ruyi* (good luck and best wishes)" in relief. The reserve is inscribed with Tibetan mantra in vermilion ink, implying the connection between man and god as well as warding off ill luck.

鎏金"消灾延寿"钱（2枚）

明万历
北京市昌平区明十三陵定陵出土
直径5厘米
明十三陵博物馆藏

Gilded coins carved with "*Xiaozai Yanshou (dispelling bad lucks and prolonging life)*" (2 pcs)

Wanli reign of Ming Dynasty
Unearthed from the Dingling Mausoleum of the Ming Tombs in Changping District, Beijing
Diameter 5 cm
The Ming Tombs Museum

这两枚金钱不是明代的流通货币，而是专为随葬而制作的，放在帝后的尸体下面，有辟邪压胜之意，也叫压胜钱。定陵出土的金钱共有117枚，全部出自帝后棺内。此两枚出自孝端后的单褥上，有"消灾延寿"四字。

These two coins were not circulating currency in the Ming Dynasty, but were specially made as burial objects. They were placed under the bodies of the emperor and empresses, with the intention of warding off evil spirits, also known as "amulet coins". A total of 117 coins unearthed from Dingling Mausoleum were all found in the coffins of the emperor and empresses. These two pieces were found in the bed sheets of Empress Xiaoduan, carved with four characters "*Xiaozai Yanshou (dispelling bad luck and prolonging life)*".

正面
The Front

背面
The Back

正面
The Front

背面
The Back

木俑

明万历
北京市昌平区明十三陵定陵出土
高 25.3、肩宽 5.1、底宽 4.77 厘米
明十三陵博物馆藏

Wooden figurine

Wanli reign of Ming Dynasty

Unearthed from the Dingling Mausoleum of the Ming Tombs
in Changping District, Beijing

Height 25.3 cm, Width of Shoulder 5.1 cm, Width of Bottom
4.77 cm

The Ming Tombs Museum

　　俑一般做成人或动物的形象，是人或动物殉葬的替代物。最早的俑是用茅草扎束而略具人形，后来以陶、木最为多见，形式有文官俑、武将俑、仪仗俑、侍俑、伎乐俑、马或骆驼等动物俑。

　　定陵出土木俑上千件，保存下来的仅三百多件，分为人俑和马俑。明朝从太祖朱元璋到明宣宗四代皇帝均有妃嫔殉葬之制，其后英宗遗诏止殉，终明之世再没有出现人殉。定陵出土木俑中的人俑，均为宫廷宦官、皂隶等内官形象，它表明皇帝死后，在阴间仍有众多内官服侍。

Figurines are usually made into human or animal figures to serve as their substitutes to be buried with the dead. The earliest figurines were tied into humanoid shapes with thatches. Later, pottery and wooden figurines prevailed and were made into the figures of civil and military officials, honor of guards, attendants, musicians, and horses or camels or other animals figures.

Over a thousand wooden figurines were unearthed from the Dingling Mausoleum, of which only over 300 have been preserved, mostly are human figurines and horse figurines. From Emperor Taizu Zhu Yuanzhang to Emperor Xuanzong of Ming, the four generations of the emperors of the Ming Dynasty had their consorts and concubines buried alive with them after they died. The practice was stopped after Emperor Yingzong forbade it in his posthumous edict. The wooden human figurines unearthed from the Dingling Mausoleum are all images of palace eunuchs, yamen runners, and other palace servants, indicating that the emperor's afterlife is still attended by many servants.

木俑

明万历
北京市昌平区明十三陵定陵出土
高 26.8、肩宽 4.1、底宽 4.5 厘米
明十三陵博物馆藏

Wooden figurine

Wanli reign of Ming Dynasty

Unearthed from the Dingling Mausoleum of the Ming Tombs
in Changping District, Beijing

Height 26.8 cm, Width of Shoulder 4.1 cm, Width of Bottom
4.5 cm

The Ming Tombs Museum

木俑

明万历
北京市昌平区明十三陵定陵出土
高 29.3、肩宽 3.9、底宽 5.4 厘米
明十三陵博物馆藏

Wooden figurine

Wanli reign of Ming Dynasty

Unearthed from the Dingling Mausoleum of the Ming Tombs
in Changping District, Beijing

Height 29.3 cm, Width of Shoulder 3.9 cm, Width of Bottom
5.4 cm

The Ming Tombs Museum

木俑

明万历
北京市昌平区明十三陵定陵出土
高 20.4、肩宽 3.3、底宽 3.15 厘米
明十三陵博物馆藏

Wooden figurine

Wanli reign of Ming Dynasty

Unearthed from the Dingling Mausoleum of the Ming Tombs
in Changping District, Beijing

Height 20.4 cm, Width of Shoulder 3.3 cm, Width of Bottom
3.15 cm

The Ming Tombs Museum

万历朝后期，政治局面呈衰落之象，而文化与艺术依旧蓬勃发展。这一时期的工艺品中，有日常生活的实用之物，也有把玩鉴赏的艺术之作；有内廷制作的皇家器具，也有民间匠人的手工艺品。这些具有鲜明时代特色的器物，为我们探寻明朝的社会生活和文化艺术打开了一扇窗户，让我们看到一个多彩而充满个性的晚明。

In the late Wanli reign, the political situation was in decline, while culture and arts continued to flourish. The handicrafts of this period included those for daily practical use and artistic works for playing and appreciation; the imperial utensils made by the imperial court and the handicrafts by folk craftsmen. These artifacts with distinctive characteristics of the times have opened a window for us to explore the social life as well as culture and arts of the Ming Dynasty, allowing us to see the colorful and full personality of the late Ming Dynasty.

第二单元

里坤物乾

一 器与用

　　以器为用，器以载道。明朝宫廷内府荟萃了全国各地的能工巧匠，生产着皇室吃穿用度所需的各类产品。为保质保量地完成宫廷需求，工匠们可以不惜工本、不计时间地使产品达到当时最高的工艺水平。定陵出土文物中，随葬的金银器多为实用器，种类齐全，或为帝后生前所使用的器具。

Utensils are for use and for expressing ideas. The Ming Dynasty's imperial storehouse gathered skilled craftsmen from all over the country, making various products for the imperial household to meet their daily needs. To guarantee the quality and quantity, the craftsmen spared no efforts to create products for the palace regardless of cost and time so they could achieve the highest level of art. Among the cultural relics unearthed from the Dingling Mausoleum, most of the buried gold and silver ware are of practical value or utensils used by emperors and empresses during their lifetime, with great variety.

明代宫廷宴饮

Palace Banquets of Ming Dynasty

明代宫廷宴饮有大宴、中宴、常宴、小宴之分，明代宴礼对各种宴会有详尽规定。在宴会中要严明等级，显示皇帝至上权威。首先是规定宴会的规模，"天子"祭天仪式后的庆成宴是最重要的大宴，可多达二千五百桌，上万人同时用餐。其次是规定宴会座次排位，万历《大明会典》中，根据宗法关系、爵位官职等，对宫廷宴饮的礼仪、座次、乐舞、饮食都有详细规定。筵宴中的每一次行酒始终伴随着乐舞，其内容多为歌颂君主圣德、皇朝一统或太平盛世。宫廷宴饮中使用的器物如金爵、金杯、金勺等器具，无一不展示着皇家风采。

Palace banquets in the Ming Dynasty were divided into grand, medium, regular, and small banquets. The banquet rites had detailed regulations for various banquets. A banquet must be arranged according to hierarchy to demonstrate the supreme authority of the emperor. Firstly, the scale of the banquet should be specified. The celebration banquet after the "Son of Heaven" completed the sacrificial rituals to heaven was the most important grand banquet of all, with up to 2,500 tables and tens of thousands of people dining at the same time. Secondly, the seating arrangement. *Collected Statutes of the Ming Dynasty* has a detailed account of the rules for the etiquette, order of seats, music and dance, and diet of palace banquets based on patriarchal relationships, titles, and official positions. Every round of the toasting during the banquet was always accompanied by music and dance, mostly to praise the monarch's virtues, the unification of the imperial dynasty, or the prosperous times. The utensils used in palace banquets, such as gold *Jue* (wine vessel), gold cups, gold spoons, and so on, all displayed the imperial style.

鎏金酒注

明万历
北京市昌平区明十三陵定陵出土
通高 16、口径 4.1、底径 5.7 厘米
明十三陵博物馆藏

Gilded wine dropper

Wanli reign of Ming Dynasty

Unearthed from the Dingling Mausoleum of the Ming Tombs
in Changping District, Beijing

Overall Height 16 cm, Mouth Diameter 4.1 cm,

Bottom Diameter 5.7 cm

The Ming Tombs Museum

直口，短颈，扁圆腹，圆筒形高足，耳形把，细短流。覆盆形圆钮盖。盖钮以金链与把上所附环钮相连。酒注是斟酒用具，大约始于唐代，自元代起，形制变化，并称之为"执壶"。但定陵出土的酒注和执壶是有区别的，主要区别在于酒注是圆筒形高圈足，而执壶是矮圈足，腹部在下。

The ewer has a straight mouth, a short neck, an oblate belly, a cylindrical high ring foot, an ear-shaped lug, a thin and short spout, and a raspberry-shaped cover with a round knob. The knob is connected to the loop button attached to the lug with a gold chain. The *Jiuzhu* (wine dropper) is a utensil for pouring wine and was dated back to the Tang Dynasty. Since the Yuan Dynasty, its shape has changed and called as "*Zhihu* (ewer)". But it is different between the *Jiuzhu* and *Zhihu* unearthed in the Dingling Mausoleum, with the former a cylindrical high ring foot, and the latter a short ring foot with the belly beneath.

鎏金梨形执壶

明万历
北京市昌平区明十三陵定陵出土
通高 10.1、口径 3、圈足径 4.1 厘米
明十三陵博物馆藏

Gilded pear-shaped handle ewer

Wanli reign of Ming Dynasty

Unearthed from the Dingling Mausoleum of the Ming Tombs
in Changping District, Beijing

Overall Height 10.1 cm, Mouth Diameter 3 cm,
Diameter of Ring Foot 4.1 cm

The Ming Tombs Museum

鎏金执壶

明万历
北京市昌平区明十三陵定陵出土
通高 15、口径 3.9、圈足径 5.2 厘米
明十三陵博物馆藏

Gilded handle ewer

Wanli reign of Ming Dynasty

Unearthed from the Dingling Mausoleum of the Ming Tombs
in Changping District, Beijing

Overall Height 15 cm , Mouth Diameter 3.9 cm,
Diameter of Ring Foot 5.2 cm

The Ming Tombs Museum

鎏金尊（附匙勺一组）

明万历
北京市昌平区明十三陵定陵出土
尊高 9.2、口径 8.1、底径 5.7 厘米；漏勺长 13.2 厘米；
勺长 13.1 厘米；匙长 15.2 厘米
明十三陵博物馆藏

Gilded *Zun* (with a set of spoons)

Wanli reign of Ming Dynasty

Unearthed from the Dingling Mausoleum of the Ming Tombs in Changping District, Beijing

Zun: Height 9.2 cm, Mouth Diameter 8.1 cm, Bottom Diameter 5.7 cm; Length of Spoon-shaped Strainer 13.2 cm; Length of Ladle 13.1 cm; Length of Small Spoon 15.2 cm

The Ming Tombs Museum

颈、腹、圈足先各自分制，后焊接在一起。内有漏勺一把，把中部有弦纹六道，勺上镂孔十三个；勺一把，形同漏勺；匙二把，舌形。

The neck, belly, and ring foot of the *Zun* were made separately first and then soldered together. Inside the *zun*, there is a colander, with six bow-string patterns in the middle of the handle and thirteen hallow carved holes on the spoon; a ladle of a similar shape to the strainer; two spoons in tongue shape.

鎏金素杯

明万历
北京市昌平区明十三陵定陵出土
高 5.5、口径 8.5、底径 3.7 厘米
明十三陵博物馆藏

Gilded plain cup

Wanli reign of Ming Dynasty

Unearthed from the Dingling Mausoleum of the Ming Tombs
in Changping District, Beijing

Height 5.5 cm, Mouth Diameter 8.5 cm,
Bottom Diameter 3.7 cm

The Ming Tombs Museum

　　定陵出土的金器以酒具最精美，有爵、注、执壶、尊、杯等。史料记载，张居正曾作《酒告篇》指出宴饮过度会荒废政务，损害健康。万历也多次发生酗酒失德事件，张居正为其代写"罪己诏"。万历十七年雒于仁上疏指出神宗有酒、色、财、气四种病症。酒具的出土不仅反映了明代酒具的风貌，也是万历皇帝好酒的证据。

Among the gold artifacts unearthed from the Dingling Mausoleum, the most exquisite ones are wine vessels, including *Jue*, *Zhu* (dropper), *Zhihu* (ewer), *Zun*, cups, etc. According to historical records, Zhang Juzheng once wrote *Admonishing on Excessive Wine (Jiu Gao Pian)*, stating that excessive banqueting would lead to neglecting government affairs and bad health. Wanli Emperor also transgressed many times for overdrinking. Zhang Juzheng wrote a "Self-Blame Edict (*Zui Ji Zhao*)" on his behalf. In the 17th year of Wanli, Luo Yuren submitted a memorial to the throne pointing out that Emperor Shenzhong was troubled by four diseases: alcohol, sex, wealth and temper. The excavation of wine vessels not only reflects the style and features of Ming Dynasty's wine set, but also serves as evidence of Wanli Emperor's alcoholism.

鎏金素杯

明万历

北京市昌平区明十三陵定陵出土

高 5.5、口径 8.5、底径 3.7 厘米

明十三陵博物馆藏

Gilded plain cup

Wanli reign of Ming Dynasty

Unearthed from the Dingling Mausoleum of the Ming Tombs
in Changping District, Beijing

Height 5.5 cm, Mouth Diameter 8.5 cm,

Bottom Diameter 3.7 cm

The Ming Tombs Museum

万历款金匙

明万历

北京市昌平区明十三陵定陵出土

长 26.5 厘米

明十三陵博物馆藏

Gold spoon with the mark of Wanli

Wanli reign of Ming Dynasty

Unearthed from the Dingling Mausoleum of the Ming Tombs
in Changping District, Beijing

Length 26.5 cm

The Ming Tombs Museum

下部呈椭圆形，柄细长，柄中部刻弦纹六道。上部刻铭文"大明万历庚申年银作局制金匙一把重二两"。

Oval-shaped lower part, slender handle, with six bow-string patterns engraved in the middle of the handle. The upper part of the handle is engraved with the inscription "A gold spoon with a weight of two taels made by the Silverwork Bureau in the Gengshen year of Wanli reign of Great Ming (1620)".

鎏金银铜勺

明万历
北京市昌平区明十三陵定陵出土
长 15.2、勺径 4.3 厘米
明十三陵博物馆藏

Gilded copper spoon

Wanli reign of Ming Dynasty

Unearthed from the Dingling Mausoleum of the Ming Tombs
in Changping District, Beijing

Length 15.2 cm, Diameter of Spoon 4.3 cm

The Ming Tombs Museum

下部呈圆形，柄上部扁平，稍弯。勺内壁鎏银，外壁及柄鎏金。

Round-shaped lower part, flat and slightly curved upper part of the handle. The inner wall of the spoon is gilded with silver, and the outer wall and handle are gilded with gold.

箸文化

Chopsticks Culture

　　"箸"便是筷子，因为"箸"与"住"谐音，有停止之意，古人认为不吉利，就反其意称为"快"，又因它大多竹制，故称为"筷子"。我国古时的筷子大多用竹子制成，"筷"与"箸"都是竹字头就是明证，但也有用木材制成的。后来，随着社会生产力的发展，封建帝王和贵族们为了体现其地位与财富，又采用金、银、玉、象牙等名贵材料制成筷子。

In Chinese, "*Zhu*" means chopsticks. As "*Zhu*" shares a homophonic sound with "*Zhu*" (stay, cease, stop), which implied infelicity to the ancients, who took the opposite meaning and referred to it as "*Kuai* (fast, quick)", and because it was mostly made of bamboo, it was called "*Kuaizi* (chopsticks)". In ancient China, chopsticks were mostly made of bamboo, which can be verified by the top radical of "*Zhu* (bamboo)" in both "*Kuai*" and "*Zhu*", but some of them were made of wood too. Later, with the development of social productivity, chopsticks made of precious materials such as gold, silver, jade, and ivory were produced for feudal emperors and nobles to highlight their status and wealth.

万历款金箸（一双）

明万历
北京市昌平区明十三陵定陵出土
长 26.1 厘米
明十三陵博物馆藏

Gold chopsticks with the mark of Wanli (1 pair)

Wanli reign of Ming Dynasty

Unearthed from the Dingling Mausoleum of the Ming Tombs in Changping District, Beijing

Length 26.1 cm

The Ming Tombs Museum

　　每箸上部刻铭文"大明万历庚申年银作局制金箸一根重二两"。

The upper part of each chopstick is engraved with the inscription "A gold chopstick with a weight of two taels made by the Silverwork Bureau in the Gengshen year of Wanli reign of Great Ming (1620)".

包金龙首木筷（一双）

明万历
北京市昌平区明十三陵定陵出土
长 21.7 厘米
明十三陵博物馆藏

Gold-plated wooden chopsticks decorated with dragon head (1 pair)

Wanli reign of Ming Dynasty

Unearthed from the Dingling Mausoleum of the Ming Tombs in Changping District, Beijing

Length 21.7 cm

The Ming Tombs Museum

日常用具

Daily Utensils

　　定陵出土的宫廷日常器用包括盒器、漱盂、碗罐、梳妆用具等，器物虽小，以小见大，包罗万象，在具备实用性的同时，亦作为明代艺术文化的载体，呈现其作为器物本身独具的魅力和神韵。一梳一洗，一盂一漱，这些看似繁琐复杂的日常起居流程，反映了古人对于生活的时尚品味和艺术追求。

The daily palace utensils unearthed from the Dingling Mausoleum include boxes, cuspidors, bowls, pots, toilet sets, etc. Small they are, yet they are a window to see big and are all-encompassing. These utensils not only had practical purposes, but also served as the vehicle of the art and culture of the Ming Dynasty, presenting their unique charm and glamour. Using specific daily utensils from morning dressing up to retiring to bed in the evening, the seemingly tedious and complicated living style reflected the fashion taste and artistic pursuit of ancient people for life.

鎏金漱盂

明万历
北京市昌平区明十三陵定陵出土
高 5.5、口径 14、底径 11.2 厘米
明十三陵博物馆藏

Gilded cuspidor

Wanli reign of Ming Dynasty

Unearthed from the Dingling Mausoleum of the Ming Tombs
in Changping District, Beijing

Height 5.5 cm, Mouth Diameter 14 cm,
Bottom Diameter 11.2 cm

The Ming Tombs Museum

银鎏金云龙纹漱盂

明万历
北京市昌平区明十三陵定陵出土
高 5.9、口径 14.3、底径 11.7 厘米
明十三陵博物馆藏

Silver gilded cuspidor with cloud and dragon design

Wanli reign of Ming Dynasty

Unearthed from the Dingling Mausoleum of the Ming Tombs in Changping District, Beijing

Height 5.9 cm, Mouth Diameter 14.3 cm, Bottom Diameter 11.7cm

The Ming Tombs Museum

　　外壁压刻龙赶珠及海水江崖云纹沙地，内底沙地压刻二龙戏珠及云纹。外底刻铭文三行："大明万历辛丑年银作局制八成色矿金沙地云龙漱盂一个重十两 / 经管官蔡奉 / 银匠杨宗礼"。

The outer wall is carved with the design of dragon chasing pearls, and stylized waves and mountain peaks on sandy ground, while the inner bottom is carved with the design of two dragons playing with a pearl and cloud pattern on sandy ground. The outer bottom is carved with the inscription in three lines: "An 80% gold content sandy ground cuspidor with the cloud and dragon design and a weight of ten taels made by the Silverwork Bureau in the Xinchou year of Wanli reign of Great Ming (1601), by administrator Cai Feng and silversmith Yang Zongli".

鎏金方盒

明万历
北京市昌平区明十三陵定陵出土
高 2.8、宽 5.6 厘米
明十三陵博物馆藏

Gilded square box

Wanli reign of Ming Dynasty

Unearthed from the Dingling Mausoleum of the Ming Tombs
in Changping District, Beijing

Height 2.8 cm, Width 5.6 cm

The Ming Tombs Museum

鎏金方盒

鎏金皂盒

明万历
北京市昌平区明十三陵定陵出土
外层高 4.6、口径 9.9、底径 8.5 厘米；
内层高 3.4、口径 10、底径 8.1 厘米
明十三陵博物馆藏

Gilded soap box

Wanli reign of Ming Dynasty

Unearthed from the Dingling Mausoleum of the Ming Tombs
in Changping District, Beijing

Outer Layer: Height 4.6 cm, Mouth Diameter 9.9 cm,
Bottom Diameter 8.5 cm;

Inner Layer: Height 3.4 cm, Mouth Diameter 10 cm,
Bottom Diameter 8.1 cm

The Ming Tombs Museum

出自万历皇帝的棺内。圆筒分为内外两层，外层中部有一周腰箍，内层底部有七个漏孔，便于使用后的肥皂残水流到外层盒的底部。出土时盒内还留有两块黑色圆形有机物。

Unearthed from Wanli Emperor's coffin, the tube-shaped box is divided into inner and outer layers, with a waist hoop in the middle of the outer layer and seven holes at the bottom of the inner layer, making it easy for soap residual water to flow to the bottom of the outer box after use. Two pieces of black round organic compound were still retained in the box at the time of excavation.

银鎏金二龙戏珠纹扳沿盆

明万历
北京市昌平区明十三陵定陵出土
高 7.6、口径 32.8、底径 23.3 厘米
明十三陵博物馆藏

Glided silver basin with folded brim and a design of two dragons playing with a pearl

Wanli reign of Ming Dynasty

Unearthed from the Dingling Mausoleum of the Ming Tombs in Changping District, Beijing

Height 7.6 cm, Mouth Diameter 32.8 cm,
Bottom Diameter 23.3 cm

The Ming Tombs Museum

出自万历皇帝的棺内。沿面刻饰两组对称的二龙戏珠纹，龙之间刻山水和云纹。盆底内壁亦为二龙戏珠和云纹，中心的半圆球则象征火珠，尤为形象生动。盆底中心部分刻铭文一周："万历年造六成五色金重二十七两三钱五分"。

Unearthed from Wanli Emperor's coffin. The folded rim is carved with two groups of symmetrical design of two dragons playing with a pearl, and the design of landscape and clouds is carved between the dragons. The inner bottom of the basin is also adorned with the design of two dragons playing with a pearl and clouds, while the semicircle ball in the center symbolizes a pearl, extremely lifelike. A ring of inscription is engraved on the central part of the outer bottom of the basin: "Made in the Wanli reign, 65% gold content, 27 taels and 3.5 cents in weight".

鎏金单柄罐

明万历
北京市昌平区明十三陵定陵出土
通高 18.4、口径 9.3、底径 10.1 厘米
明十三陵博物馆藏

Gilded pot with a single handle

Wanli reign of Ming Dynasty

Unearthed from the Dingling Mausoleum of the Ming Tombs in Changping District, Beijing

Overall Height 18.4 cm, Mouth Diameter 9.3 cm, Bottom Diameter 10.1 cm

The Ming Tombs Museum

　　出自万历皇帝棺内。底部刻铭文一周："大明万历年御用监造八成五色金重二十二两四钱"，腹部刻"尚冠上用"四字。器物的表面有磕碰和磨损，使用痕迹明显，木柄黑光发亮，可能是经长期烟熏所致。万历皇帝一生体弱多病，经常服药。这件带柄罐或为万历皇帝生前煎药用的药罐。明代皇帝患病煎服药物，有严格的制度和规定，经御医诊治后，计药开方，用金罐煎之。定陵出土药罐为研究宫廷医学提供了重要的实物资料。

Unearthed from Wanli Emperor's coffin, the pot is carved with a ring of inscription at the bottom: "Made by the Imperial Workshop in the Wanli reign of Great Ming, 85% gold content, 22 taels and 4 cents in weight." "*Shang Guan Shang Yong*" four characters are engraved on the belly. The abrasions on the surface indicate that the object had been extensively used. The wooden handle looks black and shiny, which could be the result of long-term smoking. Wanli Emperor was weak and sickly throughout his life, and taking medicine was almost a routine. This pot with a handle might be the pot decorating herbal medicine for Wanli Emperor when he was alive. There were strict systems and regulations for decocting and taking medicine for Ming Dynasty emperors when they got sick. The medicine usually was decocted in a gold pot according to the prescription of the imperial physicians after they made the diagnosis and treatment. This pot unearthed from the Dingling Mausoleum provides important material in kind for the study of palace medicine.

粉盒

Powder Boxes

古代的粉盒也叫香盒、油盒、黛盒，用于存放脂粉和香粉，跟胭脂盒有相似作用，属于古代女子日用的生活妆奁用品。粉盒由盖和底两部分组成，子母口相互扣严。中国古代女子使用妆粉最早可追溯至战国时期，流行于唐代，宋代已经出口大量粉盒瓷器，可见粉盒在当时已成为古代女子生活的日常用品。粉盒的形状有圆形、椭圆形、方形、四边形等，质地多样，早期以瓷器为主，后期出现金、银、漆器、玉石等材质。

明代李时珍在《本草纲目·燕脂》中，将当时的胭脂按原料分为四种，分别是红蓝花汁染胡粉、山燕脂花汁染粉、山榴花汁制成和紫矿染绵。其中第四种乃是上品，第二种次之，红花和山榴花汁染成的再次之。

The ancient powder boxes, also known as perfume boxes, cream boxes, or eyebrow liner boxes, were used to store cosmetics and face powder, functioning similarly to the rouge boxes, all belonging to the daily toilet set essential for women in ancient times. A powder box consists of a cover and a container that tightly fits in with each other. The earliest use of face powder by ancient Chinese women can be traced back as early as the Warring States period and became a fashion in the Tang Dynasty. By the Song Dynasty, a large number of powder porcelain boxes had been exported overseas, indicating that powder boxes were already a daily necessity for ancient women at that time. The powder boxes were made into round, oval, square, rectangle, and other different shapes in various textures. The material used was porcelain in the early stage, later powder boxes made of gold, silver, lacquerware, and jade appeared.

Li Shizhen of the Ming Dynasty divided the raw materials for making rouge into four categories in his *Compendium of Materia Medica: Rouge* - lead powder dyed of red and blue pollen, powder dyed of mountain flower extraction, cotton dyed of mountain pomegranate juice and purple minerals. The fourth category is the top-grade, followed by the second category, and the lowest grade is the one made with red flowers and pomegranate juice.

鎏金香盒

明万历
北京市昌平区明十三陵定陵出土
高 5.6、口径 16.6、底径 16.9 厘米
明十三陵博物馆藏

Gilded powder box

Wanli reign of Ming Dynasty

Unearthed from the Dingling Mausoleum of the Ming Tombs
in Changping District, Beijing

Height 5.6 cm, Mouth Diameter 16.6 cm, Bottom Diameter
16.9cm

The Ming Tombs Museum

器底刻铭文"大明万历庚申年银作局制金香盒一个重二十两"。

The inscription on the bottom of the box reads: "A gold powder box with a weight of 20 taels made by the Silverwork Bureau in the Gengshen year of Wanli reign of Great Ming (1620)".

万历年制青花云龙纹瓷盒

明万历

北京市昌平区明十三陵定陵出土

通高 2.4、口径 3.2 厘米

明十三陵博物馆藏

Blue-and-white porcelain box with the cloud and dragon design

Wanli reign of Ming Dynasty

Unearthed from the Dingling Mausoleum of the Ming Tombs in Changping District, Beijing

Overall Height 2.4 cm, Mouth Diameter 3.2 cm

The Ming Tombs Museum

出自孝端皇后棺内漆盒。盒，子母口，斜直壁，平底内凹形成圈足。盖，弧形面。白地青花，盒外壁及盖外缘各饰二行龙及海水江崖，盖面一升龙。底外壁有"大明万历年制"款。出土时盒内盛有红褐色块状物，似为胭脂。

Unearthed from the lacquered box inside Empress Xiaoduan's coffin. Box: plug-type mouth, oblique straight wall, indented flat bottom forming the ring foot. Cover: arc-shaped cover. White ground blue pattern. The outer wall of the box and the outer edge of the cover are decorated with two flying dragons designs and stylized waves and mountain peaks, with a rising dragon on the cover. The outer wall of the bottom is inscribed: "Made in the Wanli Reign of Great Ming". The box contained a reddish-brown substance at the time of excavation, which seemed to be rouge.

仿汉规矩纹铜镜

明万历
北京市昌平区明十三陵定陵出土
直径 20.2、边厚 0.5 厘米
明十三陵博物馆藏

Copper mirror with "TLV" design in imitation of Han style

Wanli reign of Ming Dynasty
Unearthed from the Dingling Mausoleum of the Ming Tombs in Changping District, Beijing
Diameter 20.2 cm, Thickness of Edge 0.5 cm
The Ming Tombs Museum

出于孝端后棺内西北角最上层，放在盛放梳妆用具的漆盒上边，背面贴在金地彩绘镜架上。同出的还有放念珠的小圆漆盒及抿子匣等。所有这些用品被一件黄色薄绢织物包裹在一起。

镜为圆钮，圆座，宽缘，仿汉式规矩镜。在钮座外有一方栏，内有十二乳钉纹，栏外有八乳，并有"T""L"记号，其间饰万字及兽纹，边缘为锯齿纹和变形云纹。方栏内十二乳之间有铭文一周，字迹模糊，似为十二地支。内区边缘亦有铭文一周，字迹亦不可辨认。

仿古倾向于学习和借鉴，是对古人艺术之美的追慕与敬畏。在历代仿古镜中，仿汉镜最多，仿唐镜次之。研究资料表明，明代仿古镜多为原镜翻模，所以纹饰大多不够清晰。另外，明代仿古镜在模仿汉唐铜镜纹饰的基础上，还增加了商标铭文，如"张家造"等。

Unearthed from the top layer of the northwest corner of Empress Xiaoduan's coffin. It was placed on top of the lacquered box of the toilet set. Its back leaned on a mirror frame painted on golden ground. The mirror was found with a small round lacquered box to contain prayer beads and a hairbrush casket at the time of excavation, all of which were wrapped together in a yellow chiffon fabric.

The mirror has a round knob, a round seat, a wide brink, and is a mirror with "TLV" design in imitation of the Han style. The knob is enclosed in a square, in which there are twelve nipple patterns. Outside the square, there are eight nipple patterns and the marks of "T" and "L", where swastika and beast designs are decorated in between. The edges are saw-tooth design and stylized cloud patterns. A ring of inscription between the twelve nipple patterns is carved in the square, but is indiscernible, seems to be the twelve earthly branches. There is also a ring of inscription around the edge of the inner area, but entirely indiscernible.

Antiquing aims to learn and draw inspiration is a kind of appreciation and reverence for the beauty of ancient art. Among the antiqued mirrors of all dynasties, most of them were modelled after the Han mirrors and Tang mirrors. Research data shows that most of the antique mirrors of the Ming Dynasty were the rollovers of the original mirrors, so the patterns were mostly not clear enough. In addition, on the basis of imitating the patterns of Han and Tang copper mirrors, the Ming antiqued mirrors also added trademark inscriptions such as "Made by the Zhang Family".

玉篦子

明万历
北京市昌平区明十三陵定陵出土
长 6、宽 3.4 厘米
明十三陵博物馆藏

Jade fine-tooth comb

Wanli reign of Ming Dynasty

Unearthed from the Dingling Mausoleum of the Ming Tombs
in Changping District, Beijing

Length 6 cm, Width 3.4 cm

The Ming Tombs Museum

　　出自万历帝棺内漆盒。篦架用白玉制成，上嵌竹齿。出土时仅存篦架，齿缺失。

Unearthed from the lacquered box inside Wanli Emperor's coffin. The comb frame is made of white jade and is embedded with bamboo teeth, which were lost at the time of excavation.

牛角梳

明万历
北京市昌平区明十三陵定陵出土
长 11.7、宽 4.3 厘米
明十三陵博物馆藏

Ox-horn comb

Wanli reign of Ming Dynasty

Unearthed from the Dingling Mausoleum of the Ming Tombs
in Changping District, Beijing

Length 11.7 cm, Width 4.3 cm

The Ming Tombs Museum

　　出自孝端后棺内漆盒，一共两件。梳为月牙形，用整支牛角刮削制成，呈褐色。此件，梳齿细密，共有梳齿七十八根。

Unearthed from the lacquered box inside the coffin of Emperess Xiaoduan, altogether two combs. The comb is crescent-shaped and made by scraping the ox horn, in brown color. This piece has fine and dense comb teeth, with a total of 78 comb teeth.

二 技与赏

　　明代社会分工精细，各类手工业空前发展，不仅表现在手工制品种类丰富多样，更表现在讲究设计，艺术性得到高度重视，制作工艺繁复而精湛。以万历时期为代表的明晚期，金银、玉石、陶瓷、织绣等各类手工艺品琳琅满目，造型丰富多彩、纹饰繁复精细，给予器物使用者日常实用性的同时，以更多的艺术享受。

In the Ming Dynasty, various handicrafts developed unprecedentedly with the division of labor, which was not only reflected in the rich and diverse kinds of handicrafts, but also in the emphasis on design, the concentration on artistry, and the sophisticated and exquisite production technology. In the late Ming Dynasty, represented by the Wanli reign, various handicrafts such as gold and silver, jade, ceramics, brocade and embroidery were dazzling, with rich and colorful shapes and elaborate decorations providing users with daily practicality and more artistic enjoyment.

镶珠宝金托金爵

明万历
北京市昌平区明十三陵定陵出土
通高 10.3、爵长径 9.6 厘米；托口径 15.9、底径 13.1
厘米
明十三陵博物馆藏

Gold *Jue* with gold tray inlaid with gems

Wanli reign of Ming Dynasty

Unearthed from the Dingling Mausoleum of the Ming Tombs
in Changping District, Beijing

Overall Height 10.3 cm; *Jue*: Mouth Diameter 9.6 cm;

Tray: Mouth Diameter 15.9 cm, Bottom Diameter 13.1 cm

The Ming Tombs Museum

爵腹外壁压刻半浮雕式的二龙戏珠及海水江崖流
云纹，三足及二柱刻龙首纹，把饰云雷纹，三足上部
及二柱顶端各嵌红宝石一块。底外壁一周刻字"万历
年造足色金重五两一钱七分"。

托盘中心立一树墩形柱，三面分别雕出花瓶形，
瓶内各插一支嵌有珠宝的花卉。口沿及腹内壁刻勾连
云纹，外壁饰二龙戏珠纹，底内壁刻半浮雕式的龙赶
珠及云纹，中心立柱满饰如意云头纹。插入瓶形内的
牡丹花枝除嵌有红、蓝宝石外，还饰以金银锭、珊瑚、
犀角等八宝装饰。

金爵与金托设计构思十分巧妙，造型优美，装饰
华丽，富有强烈的稳定感，具有很高的艺术价值。

The outer wall of the *Jue*'s belly is embossed with the design of
two dragons playing with a pearl and stylized waves and mountain
peaks with floating clouds in semi-relief. The three legs and two
pillars are carved with the dragon head design, and the handle is
decorated with the cloud and thunder design. The upper part of
the three legs and the top of the two pillars are each embedded
with a ruby. The outer wall at the bottom is engraved with a ring of
inscription: "Made in the Wanli Reign, pure gold, 5 taels and 1.7
cents in weight".

In the center of the tray stands a stump-shaped column, with
three sides carved in the shape of vases, each containing a flower
embedded with gems. The rim and inner wall of the belly are carved
with the interlocking cloud design; the outer wall is decorated with
two dragons playing with a pearl; the inner wall of the bottom is
embossed with the design of dragon chasing pearls and clouds in
semi-relief; the central column is decorated with the Ruyi-sceptre
design. The peony branches inserted into the "vase" are adorned
not only with rubies and sapphires, but also adorned with gold and
silver ingots, corals, rhinoceros horns, and eight treasures.

The gold *Jue* and gold tray are ingenious in design, beautiful in
modelling, and gorgeous in decorations, rendering a strong sense of
stability. It is a work with high artistic value.

镂空金盖金托玉碗

明万历

北京市昌平区明十三陵定陵出土

通高15、碗口径15.2、圈足径5.9厘米；盖口径15.7厘米；托口径20.3、底径16.7厘米

明十三陵博物馆藏

Jade bowl with gold cover and tray in openwork

Wanli reign of Ming Dynasty

Unearthed from the Dingling Mausoleum of the Ming Tombs in Changping District, Beijing

Overall Height 15 cm, Bowl: Mouth Diameter 15.2 cm, Diameter of Ring Foot 5.9 cm; Cover: Mouth Diameter 15.7 cm; Saucer: Mouth Diameter 20.3 cm, Bottom Diameter 16.7 cm

The Ming Tombs Museum

出土时位于万历帝棺内西端北侧，金玉合器。玉碗为白玉制成，细腻莹润，洁白无瑕。玉碗上盖有一个金碗盖，盖面以镂空云纹为地，上饰蛟龙赶珠纹，顶部饰一莲花形钮，中心嵌有一块红宝石。龙姿矫健优美，作腾空飞跃状。碗下有一个黄金托盘，底部正中由外壁向内压出一圈足形碗托，用来契合碗底。

The bowl was found at the north side of the western end of Wanli Emperor's coffin at the time of excavation, with a gold and jade joint. The bowl made of white jade is smooth and delicate, white and spotless. The cover is golden, with the hollow carved cloud design as the ground, and decorated with dragon-chasing pearls. The top is decorated with a lotus-shaped knob, in which a ruby is embedded in the center. The dragon looks agile and graceful as if souring into the sky. There is a gold saucer under the bowl, with a ring-foot-shaped bowl holder pressed inward from the outer wall at the center of the bottom to fit the bottom of the bowl.

金盖金碗托青花缠枝花卉纹碗

明万历

北京市昌平区明十三陵定陵出土

通高 13.5、碗口径 13.5、圈足径 5.2 厘米；盖口径
14.2 厘米；托口径 19.3、底径 16.3 厘米

明十三陵博物馆藏

Blue-and-white porcelain bowl with gold cover and tray

Wanli reign of Ming Dynasty

Unearthed from the Dingling Mausoleum of the Ming Tombs in Changping District, Beijing

Overall Height 13.5 cm, Bowl: Mouth Diameter 13.5 cm, Diameter of Ring Foot 5.2 cm; Cover: Mouth Diameter 14.2 cm; Saucer: Mouth Diameter 19.3 cm, Bottom Diameter 16.3 cm

The Ming Tombs Museum

出土时位于万历皇帝棺内西端南侧。敞口，深腹，圈足，白地青花，腹部饰缠枝四季花卉纹，近底部饰莲瓣纹，圈足饰花叶纹。瓷碗还附有金碗盖、金碗托各一件。金盖素面，直口，弧面，呈阶梯状，圆钮。口沿内侧刻铭文十四字："万历年造六成五色金重四两八钱"。金托口外侈，卷沿，浅腹，平底。底中部由外向内打出一个圆形圈足，刚好套住瓷碗圈足。底外壁中部刻铭文一周："万历年造六成五色金重八两七钱五分"。

青花碗，胎釉细腻，洁白如玉，壁薄如纸，晶莹透亮，再配以金盖、金托，更显富丽华贵。碗的边缘有使用痕迹，应是万历生前使用的食具。

Found at the southern side of the western end of Wanli Emperor's coffin at the time of excavation, the bowl has a spreading mouth, a deep belly, a ring foot, and white ground and blue patterns. The belly is decorated with the design of interlocking plants and flowers. Lotus-petal patterns are decorated near the bottom, and floral and leaf patterns are adorned on the ring foot. The porcelain bowl also comes with a gold cover and a gold tray. The gold cover has a plain surface, a straight mouth, an arc-shaped face in a ladder pattern, and a round knob. Fourteen characters are engraved on the inner side of the rim: "Made in the Wanli Reign, 65% gold content, 4 tales 8 cents in weight". The gold tray has a wide flared mouth with a spiral rim, a shallow belly, and a flat bottom. At the middle of the bottom, a circular ring foot is made from the outside to the inside, which just hitches the ring foot of the porcelain bowl. A ring of the inscription is engraved in the middle of the outer wall of the bottom: "Made in the Wanli Reign, 65% gold content, 8 taels, 7.5 cents in weight".

The blue-and-white porcelain bowl is featured with smooth and fine body glaze, jade-like color, paper-thin wall, and crystal clear and transparent appearance. Couple with the gold cover and tray, it looks even more magnificent and luxurious. From the worn-out traces at the rim of the bowl, it could be the tableware of Wanli Emperor.

鎏金工艺
Gilding Technology

　　"鎏金"是一种传统的镀金工艺，其方法是将金和水银合成"金汞剂"，涂在铜或银器表面，然后加热使水银蒸发。金在器物表面固结，形成金黄色镀层。经过鎏金处理的器物色泽金灿夺目、富丽华贵，由于覆盖在器物表面的黄金具有稳定的化学性质，鎏金器物在出土时色泽基本保存完好。

"Gilding" is a traditional gold-plating technology that involves synthesizing gold and mercury into "gold amalgam", coating it onto the surface of copper or silver vessels, and then heating it to evaporate the mercury. Gold solidifies on the surface of objects, forming a golden yellow coating. The color of the gilded objects looks dazzling and magnificent. Due to the stable chemical properties of gold plated on the surface of the objects, the gilded objects basically retained the color and luster when unearthed.

银鎏金扳沿盆

明隆庆

北京市昌平区明十三陵定陵出土

高 7.5、外径 43.6、内径 36.1、底径 30 厘米

明十三陵博物馆藏

Glided silver basin with folded rim

Longqing reign of Ming Dynasty

Unearthed from the Dingling Mausoleum of the Ming Tombs in Changping District, Beijing

Height 7.5 cm, Outer Diameter 43.6 cm, Inner Diameter 36.1 cm, Bottom Diameter 30 cm

The Ming Tombs Museum

盆底中心部分刻铭文一周："大明隆庆戊辰年造"。

A ring of inscription is carved at the center part of the bottom of the basin: "Made in the Wuchen year of Longqing reign of Great Ming (1568) ".

银鎏金寿山福海云龙纹八方粉盒

明万历
北京市昌平区明十三陵定陵出土
通高5.1、底径7.4、口径9.7、盖径9.6、粉扑径8.2
厘米
明十三陵博物馆藏

Gilded silver octagonal powder box with carved design

Wanli reign of Ming Dynasty

Unearthed from the Dingling Mausoleum of the Ming Tombs in Changping District, Beijing

Height 5.1 cm, Bottom Diameter 7.4 cm, Mouth Diameter 9.7 cm, Diameter of Cover 9.6 cm, Diameter of Powder Puff 8.2 cm

The Ming Tombs Museum

盒内装有粉扑盖一个，上刻龙戏珠纹，圆钮，周有小孔，用线缀连棉絮。器盖与器身皆为沙地，器口和盖口刻连续的变形云纹。器腹与盖壁均相应分成八格，每格刻一游龙纹。盖面刻一正面龙、海水江崖及云纹。出土时盒内残留有白色粉末，尚有余香。

A powder puff cover is encased in the box, on which it is engraved with the design of dragons playing with a pearl; a round knob, with small holes around it, and stitched with cotton wool. The cover and body of the box are both sandy grounds. The rims of the cover and box are engraved with continuous stylized cloud patterns. The belly and wall of the cover are divided into eight corresponding sections, each with a wandering dragon pattern engraved on it. The cover is carved with the design of a front facing dragon, stylized waves, mountain peaks, and clouds. There was still white powder with lingering fragrance inside at the time of excavation.

鎏金夔龙纹海棠式盘

明万历
北京市昌平区明十三陵定陵出土
高 1、长 17.1、宽 13.4 厘米
明十三陵博物馆藏

Gilded begonia-shaped plate with *Kui*-dragon design

Wanli reign of Ming Dynasty

Unearthed from the Dingling Mausoleum of the Ming Tombs in Changping District, Beijing

Height 1 cm, Length 17.1 cm, Width 13.4 cm

The Ming Tombs Museum

银鎏金盘

明万历
北京市昌平区明十三陵定陵出土
高 1.5、口径 17.3、底径 14.5 厘米
明十三陵博物馆藏

Gilded silver plate

Wanli reign of Ming Dynasty

Unearthed from the Dingling Mausoleum of the Ming Tombs
in Changping District, Beijing

Height 1.5 cm, Mouth Diameter 17.3 cm,
Bottom Diameter 14.5 cm

The Ming Tombs Museum

底内壁中心凸起一周，内刻"福"字一个，并在字和凸起部分鎏金。

The plate has a protruding circle in the center of the inner bottom,
where the character "*Fu* (blessing) " is engraved inside, with gold
plated on the character and the protruding part.

绦环

Suspension Loops

绦环是丝绦上用作带扣的圆环，使用时将丝绦的两端分别系在圆环上，宜结宜解，非常方便。其材料有金、铜、铁、玉、玛瑙等。两宋时喜用玉绦环，明代以金为时尚。古人也会在不同季节选择搭配不同的绦环，《老乞大》："系腰时也按四季：春里系金绦环；夏里系玉钩子，最低的是菜玉，最高的是羊脂玉；秋里系减金钩子，寻常的不用，都是玲珑花样的；冬里系金厢宝石闹装，又系有综（棕）眼的乌犀系腰。"

《明宫冠服仪仗图》中的诸色阔色丝扁绦与象牙雕花绦环

The varied colored silk ribbon and the ivory suspension loop carved with design from *Illustrations of Palace Costume and Imperial Insignias of Ming Dynasty*

The Suspension loop is a loop used as a belt buckle on a silk ribbon. It is to tie the two ends of the silk ribbon respectively on the ring at the time of use, easy to tie and untie, very convenient. It can be made of gold, copper, iron, jade, agate, and other materials. During the Song dynasties, jade suspension loops were favored, while during the Ming Dynasty, gold ones became the fashion. The ancients also chose to match different suspension loops in different seasons, as shown in the textbook *Kitat*: "Different seasons should wear different belts. In spring, the gold suspension loops; in summer, jade belt hooks, with the lowest grade being green jade ones and the highest mutton-fat jade ones; in autumn, gold belt hooks, but not the common ones, usually the ones with exquisite design; in winter, the belt hooks of gold inlaid with gems, or the belt hooks made of rhinoceros with a brown eye."

鎏金松鹤长方形绦环

明万历
北京市昌平区明十三陵定陵出土
长 15.4、宽 4 厘米
明十三陵博物馆藏

Gilded rectangular suspension loop

Wanli reign of Ming Dynasty

Unearthed from the Dingling Mausoleum of the Ming Tombs
in Changping District, Beijing

Length 15.4 cm, Width 4 cm

The Ming Tombs Museum

万历帝服饰。背面两端有方形花丝灵芝纹钮两个，当为结带或穿带之用。绦环正面嵌五块宝石：中间为祖母绿，左右各两块红、蓝宝石，两侧焊制流云纹并且镶嵌十二颗珍珠。背面中心嵌一个"寿"字，上部分两侧嵌松竹，下部嵌梅花、灵芝和仙鹤。四只仙鹤或作展翅欲飞状，或作回首状，或作单腿屹立，姿态各异、优美生动。

Costume of Wanli Emperor. There are two square filigreed buttons with design of glossy ganoderma on the back at either end, which should be used for tying or threading the belt. The front of the artifact is embedded with five gemstones: an emerald in the center, a ruby and a sapphire respectively on the left and right sides. The two sides are welded with flowing cloud patterns and inlaid with twelve pearls. The center of the back is embedded with the character "*Shou* (longevity)", the upper part is embedded with pine and bamboo on either side, and the lower part is embedded with plum blossoms, magic fungus, and cranes. The four cranes either spread their wings, look back, or stand on one leg, each in a different, graceful, and vivid posture.

鎏金花卉纹嵌宝石绦环

明万历
北京市昌平区明十三陵定陵出土
长 9.8、宽 4.8 厘米
明十三陵博物馆藏

Gilded suspension loop carved with design and inlaid with gemstones

Wanli reign of Ming Dynasty
Unearthed from the Dingling Mausoleum of the Ming Tombs in Changping District, Beijing
Length 9.8 cm, Width 4.8 cm
The Ming Tombs Museum

万历帝服饰。云头形，背面两端有两个葵花形圆形钮。底部由葵花、云头、银锭和"卮杯"形花纹组成底托，正面中心嵌祖母绿一块，周围及两端共嵌红宝石六块，蓝、白宝石各二块，珍珠六颗。

Costume of Wanli Emperor. The piece is in scroll-cloud shape, with two sunflower-shaped round buttons at either end of the back. The bottom is formed into a collet with designs of sunflowers, scroll clouds, silver ingots, and wine-container-shaped design. The center of the front is embedded with an emerald, with six rubies, two blue gemstones, two white gemstones, and six pearls embedded around and at both ends.

鎏金花卉纹嵌红宝石绦环

明万历

北京市昌平区明十三陵定陵出土

长 5.3、宽 4 厘米

明十三陵博物馆藏

Gilded suspension loop carved with design and inlaid with gemstones

Wanli reign of Ming Dynasty

Unearthed from the Dingling Mausoleum of the Ming Tombs in Changping District, Beijing

Length 5.3 cm, Width 4 cm

The Ming Tombs Museum

万历帝服饰。背面两端有云形钮两个，底为灵芝花及花丝组成。四壁为卷草纹，正面中心嵌红宝石一块，周围镶珍珠十四颗。

Costume of Wanli Emperor. There are two cloud-shaped round buttons at either end of the back, and the bottom is composed of magic fungus and filigrees. The four walls are floral scrolls, with a ruby embedded in the center of the front, surrounded by fourteen pearls.

鎏金花卉纹镶宝石绦环

明万历
北京市昌平区明十三陵定陵出土
长 10.3、宽 6.4 厘米
明十三陵博物馆藏

**Gilded suspension loop carved with design
and inlaid with gemstones**

Wanli reign of Ming Dynasty
Unearthed from the Dingling Mausoleum of the Ming Tombs
in Changping District, Beijing
Length 10.3 cm, Width 6.4 cm
The Ming Tombs Museum

　　万历帝服饰。心字形，背面两端有两个花丝圆形钮。
整个"心"字由上下两层花丝组成，四壁为缠枝花纹，
正面嵌猫睛石一块，红、蓝、绿、黄宝石各一块，珍
珠三颗。

Costume of Wanli Emperor. The piece is in the shape of a heart,
with two filigreed round buttons at either end of the back. The whole
character of "*Xin* (heart)" is composed of two layers of filigrees. The
four walls are decorated with the design of interlocking flowers. The
front is inlaid with a cat's-eye stone, a ruby, a sapphire, an emerald,
a topaz, and three pearls.

纽扣

Costume Accessary: Buttons

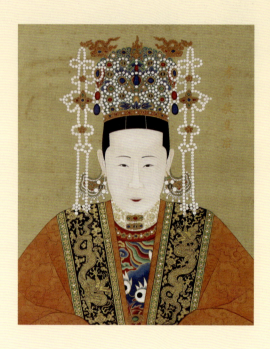

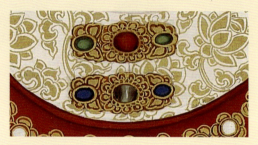

明孝宗皇后像

台北故宫博物院藏

Portrait of empress of Emperor Xiaozong of Ming
Collection of Taipei Palace Museum

　　明代开始盛行在女子上衣使用金或者鎏金镶宝纽扣，因为这一时期女子所穿对襟袄子上有竖领（或曰立领），竖领上通常使用两两成对的纽扣，成为视觉上不可忽视的装点。竖领和纽扣的出现标志着明代女子服饰的变化，即不再露出粉颈、内衣乃至抹胸。

The trend of attaching gold or gilded buttons on women's jackets began to prevail in the Ming Dynasty. As women wore center-buttoned jackets with a vertical collar (or standing collar), which often had two pairs of buttons facing each other, forming an unneglectable visual ornament. The emergence of vertical collars and buttons marked a transformation of costume for women in the Ming Dynasty, that is, they no longer had their necks, undergarments, or even strapless tops exposed.

如意云头形金纽扣

明万历
北京市昌平区明十三陵定陵出土
通长 4.92、宽 2.6 厘米
明十三陵博物馆藏

Gold button with *Ruyi-sceptre* design

Wanli reign of Ming Dynasty

Unearthed from the Dingling Mausoleum of the Ming Tombs
in Changping District, Beijing

Overall Length 4.92 cm, Width 2.6 cm

The Ming Tombs Museum

《说文》曰："纽（同'钮'），系也；一曰结而可解。"明代出现了一种子母扣式纽扣，扣子有两头，扣眼在中间以柄套环，明代这种纽扣已经首饰化，造型多采用如意形、银锭形、"卍"字形等，材质多以金、银、鎏金为主。

According to *Shuo Wen*: "*Niu* (button), for tying; also known as knot and can be untied." In the Ming Dynasty, a type of snap fasteners appeared on buttons. The button has two ends, with the buttonhole in the middle. This type of button had already become ornaments in the Ming Dynasty, which were modelled mostly in Ruyi-sceptre-shaped, the shape of silver ingot or character of "*Wan*", and were made mainly in gold, silver, gilded gold and other materials.

蝶戏花金纽扣

明万历
北京市昌平区明十三陵定陵出土
通长 4.84、宽 2.48 厘米
明十三陵博物馆藏

Gold button with design of butterflies and flowers

Wanli reign of Ming Dynasty

Unearthed from the Dingling Mausoleum of the Ming Tombs in
Changping District, Beijing

Overall Length 4.84 cm, Width 2.48 cm

The Ming Tombs Museum

童子祝寿金纽扣

明万历
北京市昌平区明十三陵定陵出土
通长 5.06、宽 2.75、童子高 1.9 厘米
明十三陵博物馆藏

Gold button decorated with two boys offering birthday congratulations

Wanli reign of Ming Dynasty
Unearthed from the Dingling Mausoleum of the Ming Tombs in Changping District, Beijing
Overall Length 5.06 cm, Width 2.75 cm,
Height of Child 1.9 cm
The Ming Tombs Museum

银锭形金纽扣

明万历
北京市昌平区明十三陵定陵出土
通长 3.76、中径 1.73 厘米
明十三陵博物馆藏

Silver-ingot-shaped gold button

Wanli reign of Ming Dynasty

Unearthed from the Dingling Mausoleum of the Ming Tombs
in Changping District, Beijing

Overall Length 3.76 cm, Width 1.73 cm

The Ming Tombs Museum

银锭形金纽扣

"喜报平安"金挂饰

明万历
北京市昌平区明十三陵定陵出土
长 8.4、宽 3.5 厘米
明十三陵博物馆藏

Gold pendant carved with double happiness and firecrackers (*Xi Bao Ping An*)

Wanli reign of Ming Dynasty
Unearthed from the Dingling Mausoleum of the Ming Tombs in Changping District, Beijing
Length 8.4 cm, Width 3.5 cm
The Ming Tombs Museum

挂饰中心镂刻双喜字,下部为瓶形,瓶上刻一"安"字,喜字两侧刻"爆竹"纹,两面纹饰相同。文字与图案共同组成吉祥纹样,寓意"喜报平安"。

The center of the pendant is engraved with two "*Xi* (double happiness)" characters, with the lower part in the shape of a bottle. The bottle is engraved with the character "*An* (safe, in good health)", and designs of firecrackers are engraved on either side of the "*Xi*" characters identically. The text and the design jointly form an auspicious pattern, symbolizing "*Xi Bao Ping An* (good news of being safe and sound)".

金簪玉坠

Gold Hairpins and Jade Pendants

明代金银首饰在类型和样式上大量增加，名称和插戴方式也愈加细化。明廷后妃佩戴首饰，一是随年节、时令不同而变更，二是遇圣寿、大喜、大典时换戴相应吉庆寓意的簪钗。定陵出土簪钗耳坠等首饰 248 件，在质料、装饰和制作工艺上极为考究，展示了明代首饰制作的辉煌，反映出了明代手工业发展的水平。定陵首饰又以簪的数量最多，质地有金、银、铜、琥珀、玳瑁、玉、木等诸种，包含打制、雕刻、累丝、琢玉、镶嵌、焊接等多种工艺，样式精细复杂。

The Ming Dynasty saw a substantial increase of gold and silver jewelry in terms of forms and styles. The way people addressed them and wore them also became more particular. The empress and imperial concubines in the Ming palace wore different jewelry on different festive occasions and seasons, as well as imperial birthdays, wedding days or grand ceremonies when wearing the corresponding auspicious symbol of the hairpin. A total of 248 pieces of jewelry including hairpins and earrings were unearthed from the Dingling Mausoleum. They are extremely exquisite in materials, decoration, and craftsmanship, reflecting the brilliance of jewelry production technology and the state of art in the Ming Dynasty. Among these, hairpins account for the largest number and their textures vary from gold, silver, copper, amber, tortoiseshell, jade and wood, etc. Made through various processes of forging, carving, filigreeing, jade carving, inlaying, and welding, they look meticulous and sophisticated in styles and forms.

嵌珠宝葫芦形金簪

明万历
北京市昌平区明十三陵定陵出土
长 6.9、径 1.9 厘米
明十三陵博物馆藏

Gourd-shaped gold hairpin inlaid with gemstones

Wanli reign of Ming Dynasty
Unearthed from the Dingling Mausoleum of the Ming Tombs in Changping District, Beijing
Length 6.9 cm, Dimeter 1.9 cm
The Ming Tombs Museum

万历帝首饰。顶端为亚腰葫芦形金托，上镶石榴子红宝石一块，珍珠一颗。

Jewelry of Wanli Emperor. The top is a gold holder in the shape of a narrow-waisted gourd, adorned with a pomegranate ruby and a pearl.

嵌红宝石金簪

明万历
北京市昌平区明十三陵定陵出土
长 8.2、径 1.3 厘米
明十三陵博物馆藏

Gold hairpin inlaid with ruby

Wanli reign of Ming Dynasty
Unearthed from the Dingling Mausoleum of the Ming Tombs in Changping District, Beijing
Length 8.2 cm, Diameter 1.3 cm
The Ming Tombs Museum

万历帝首饰。

Jewelry of Wanli Emperor.

嵌猫睛石金簪

明万历

北京市昌平区明十三陵定陵出土

长 5.3、径 1.2 厘米

明十三陵博物馆藏

Gold hairpin inlaid with cat's-eye stone

Wanli reign of Ming Dynasty

Unearthed from the Dingling Mausoleum of the Ming Tombs
in Changping District, Beijing

Length 5.3 cm, Diameter 1.2 cm

The Ming Tombs Museum

万历帝首饰。定陵出土的 56 件万历皇帝金簪中有
14 件都镶嵌有猫睛石。此簪猫睛石"一线中横，四面
活光，轮转照人"，晶莹润泽，实为罕见。

Jewelry of Wanli Emperor. Cat's-eye stone. Among the 56 pieces
of gold hairpins of Wanli Emperor unearthed from the Dingling
Mausoleum, 14 pieces are all embedded with cat's-eye stones.
This hairpin "with the pin set in the middle, shining on all sides,
mirroring people in all directions". It is crystal clear and glossy, a
real rarity.

嵌宝石"祝延万寿"款金簪

明万历
北京市昌平区明十三陵定陵出土
长 16.2、宽 1.7 厘米
明十三陵博物馆藏

Gold hairpin with inscription of "*Zhu Yan Wan Shou*" and inlaid with gems

Wanli reign of Ming Dynasty

Unearthed from the Dingling Mausoleum of the Ming Tombs in Changping District, Beijing

Length 16.2 cm, Width 1.7 cm

The Ming Tombs Museum

孝靖后首饰。

Jewelry of Empress Xiaojing.

白玉"佛"字嵌蓝宝石金簪（一对）

明万历
北京市昌平区明十三陵定陵出土
长 6.7～7、宽 2.3～2.4 厘米
明十三陵博物馆藏

Gold hairpin with jade *"Fo"* character inlaid with sapphire (1 pair)

Wanli reign of Ming Dynasty
Unearthed from the Dingling Mausoleum of the Ming Tombs in Changping District, Beijing
Length 6.7 - 7 cm, Width 2.3 - 2.4 cm
The Ming Tombs Museum

孝端后首饰。顶部饰一白玉"佛"字，下部与白玉花形饰相连，字中心嵌蓝宝石一块。

Jewelry of Emperess Xiaoduan. The top is decorated with a white jade in the form of Chinese character *"Fo* (Buddha)"，on which a sapphire is inlaid in the center; the lower part is connected to an ornament in the shape of a white jade flower.

金环宝石耳坠（一对）

明万历
北京市昌平区明十三陵定陵出土
通长 4.3、环径 1.9 ～ 2.1 厘米
明十三陵博物馆藏

Gold earring with a dangling ruby (1 pair)

Wanli reign of Ming Dynasty

Unearthed from the Dingling Mausoleum of the Ming
Tombs in Changping District, Beijing

Overall length 4.3 cm, Diameter of Ring 1.9 - 2.1 cm

The Ming Tombs Museum

孝端后首饰，下系红宝石一块。

Jewelry of Emperess Xiaoduan. The earring has a dangling ruby.

玉雕"童子持莲"嵌红宝石金簪（一对）

明万历
北京市昌平区明十三陵定陵出土
长 10.3～10.5、宽 1.4～2.2 厘米
明十三陵博物馆藏

Gold hairpin with carved jade and stringed with gems (1 pair)

Wanli reign of Ming Dynasty

Unearthed from the Dingling Mausoleum of the Ming Tombs in Changping District, Beijing

Length 10.3 - 10.5 cm, Width 1.4 - 2.2 cm

The Ming Tombs Museum

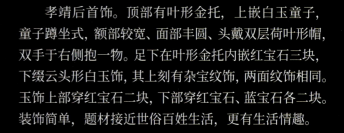

孝靖后首饰。顶部有叶形金托，上嵌白玉童子，童子蹲坐式，额部较宽、面部丰圆、头戴双层荷叶形帽，双手于右侧抱一物。足下在叶形金托内嵌红宝石三块，下缀云头形白玉饰，其上刻有杂宝纹饰，两面纹饰相同。玉饰上部穿红宝石二块，下部穿红宝石、蓝宝石各二块。装饰简单，题材接近世俗百姓生活，更有生活情趣。

Jewelry of Empress Xiaojing. The top is a leaf-shaped gold holder embedded with a white jade child in a squatting posture, who has a wide forehead, and a round face and wears a double-layer lotus-leaf-shaped hat, holding something with both hands on the right side. The gold holder under his feet is embedded with three rubies and decorated with a scroll-cloud-shaped white jade ornament below, on which it is carved with the design of miscellaneous treasures, identical on either side. The upper part of the jade ornament is stringed with two rubies, while the lower part is stringed with two rubies and two sapphires. The hairpins are full of life interests with simple decoration and the theme close to the secular life of the common people.

云鬓间的动植物世界

Hairpins Decorated with Animals and Plants

在定陵出土的金银首饰中，有不少以动植物为装饰题材的发簪，动物之属有龙、凤、仙鹤、鸳鸯、鹿、龟、兔以及蜂、蝶、草虫等，植物之属有花卉、寿果和灵芝等。明代工匠以这些动植物装饰来表达吉祥寓意，造型自然生动，富有意趣。

Among the gold and silver jewelry unearthed in the Dingling Mausoleum, there are many hairpins decorated with animals and plants, which include dragons, phoenixes, cranes, mandarin ducks, deer, turtles, rabbits, bees, butterflies, insects, and other animals, as well as flowers and plants, peaches, glossy ganoderma, and other plants. The craftsmen in the Ming Dynasty used these flora and fauna decorations to express auspicious meanings, and make their styles natural, vivid and interesting.

嵌珍珠梅化式金簪

明万历
北京市昌平区明十三陵定陵出土
长 7.2、径 1.7 厘米
明十三陵博物馆藏

Quincunx gold hairpin inlaid with pearl

Wanli reign of Ming Dynasty

Unearthed from the Dingling Mausoleum of the Ming Tombs
in Changping District, Beijing

Length 7.2 cm, Diameter 1.7 cm

The Ming Tombs Museum

万历帝首饰。顶端为五瓣梅化托，托内嵌珍珠一颗。

Jewelry of Wanli Emperor. The top is a five-petal plum blossom
holder, with a pearl inlaid inside.

白玉嵌红宝石金簪

明万历

北京市昌平区明十三陵定陵出土

长 7.6、径 2 厘米

明十三陵博物馆藏

Gold hairpin with white jade inlaid with ruby

Wanli reign of Ming Dynasty

Unearthed from the Dingling Mausoleum of the Ming Tombs in Changping District, Beijing

Length 7.6 cm, Diameter 2 cm

The Ming Tombs Museum

万历帝首饰。顶部附覆莲形白玉花金托，上嵌石榴子红宝石一颗。

Jewelry of Wanli Emperor. The top is a white jade and gold holder in lotus shape, embedded with a pomegranate ruby.

嵌紫晶兔金簪

明万历

北京市昌平区明十三陵定陵出土

长 7.1、宽 1.7 厘米

明十三陵博物馆藏

Gold hairpin inlaid with amethyst

Wanli reign of Ming Dynasty

Unearthed from the Dingling Mausoleum of the Ming Tombs
in Changping District, Beijing

Length 7.1 cm, Width 1.7 cm

The Ming Tombs Museum

万历帝首饰。万历棺中出土两件镶嵌紫晶兔金簪。
兔呈蹲伏，回首，竖耳，眼部镶绿宝石，背部有一枚
金灵芝。在中国古代，兔常代表月亮，灵芝因生长时
间久，常被认为是仙草。

Jewelry of Wanli Emperor. Two gold hairpins inlaid with an
amethyst rabbit were unearthed from Wanli Emperor's coffin. The
rabbit in a crouching position carries a glossy ganoderma on its
back, with its eyes looking back and ears erected. Its eye part is
adorned with emeralds. In ancient China, rabbits often represented
the moon, and glossy ganoderma was often considered a magic herb
due to its long growth time.

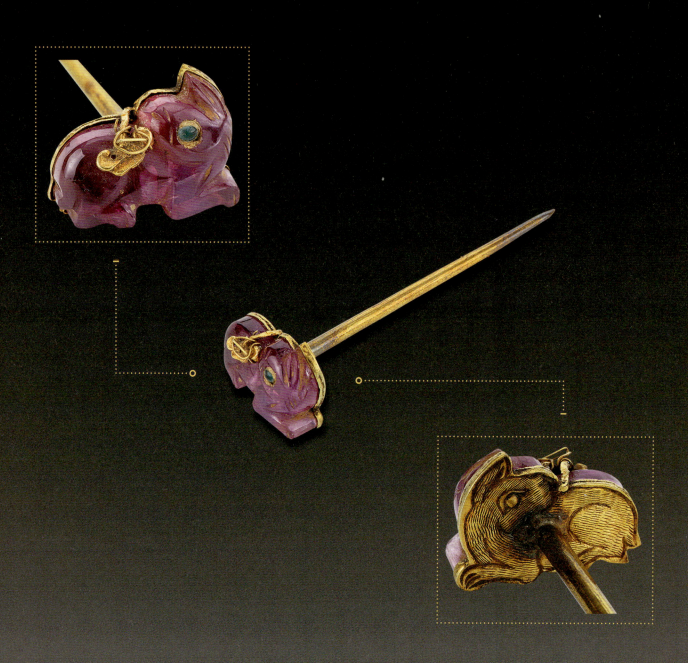

白玉嵌珠宝花蝶金簪

孝靖后首饰。

明万历
北京市昌平区明十三陵定陵出土
长 12.7、宽 4.6 厘米
明十三陵博物馆藏

Jewelry of Empress Xiaojing.

Gold hairpin with white jade inlaid with gems, flowers and butterflies

Wanli reign of Ming Dynasty

Unearthed from the Dingling Mausoleum of the Ming Tombs in Changping District, Beijing

Length 12.7 cm, Width 4.6 cm

The Ming Tombs Museum

嵌宝石刻龙纹金簪

明万历
北京市昌平区明十三陵定陵出土
长 15.5、宽 1.2 厘米
明十三陵博物馆藏

Gold hairpin inlaid with gems and carved with dragon design

Wanli reign of Ming Dynasty
Unearthed from the Dingling Mausoleum of the Ming Tombs in Changping District, Beijing
Length 15.5 cm, Width 1.2 cm
The Ming Tombs Museum

孝靖后首饰。簪的本名称"笄"（《说文》："笄，簪也。"），是古人用来绾定发髻或冠的长针，可用金属、骨头、玉石等制成。钗是由两股簪子交叉组合成的一种首饰，用来绾住头发。簪与钗的区别在于发簪作成一股，而发钗作成两股。笄首有垂珠坠饰者则称为"步摇"。

Jewelry of Empress Xiaojing. *Zan* (hairpin), originally called "*Ji*" (*Shuowen*: "*Ji* is *zan*.") is a long pin used by ancient people to secure hair buns or crowns, usually made of metal, bone, jade, and other materials. *Chai* is an ornament combining two overlapping *Zan* or hairpins to hold hair. The difference between *Zan* and *Chai* is that the former is made of one pin, while the latter is made of two pins. When a pendant is affixed to the head of *Ji*, or hairpin, it is called "*Buyao* (dangling hairpin)".

嵌宝石白玉"万"字双兔如意纹金簪

明万历
北京市昌平区明十三陵定陵出土
长 17.5、宽 2.5 厘米
明十三陵博物馆藏

Gold Hairpin with white jade carved with two
rabbits, *"Wan"* character and *Ruyi*-sceptre
design and inlaid with gems

Wanli reign of Ming Dynasty

Unearthed from the Dingling Mausoleum of the Ming Tombs
in Changping District, Beijing

Length 17.5 cm, width 2.5 cm

The Ming Tombs Museum

孝靖后首饰。

Jewelry of Empress Xiaojing.

玉雕鸳鸯嵌红宝石金簪

明万历
北京市昌平区明十三陵定陵出土
长 11、宽 2.4 厘米
明十三陵博物馆藏

Gold hairpin with jade carved mandarin duck and inlaid with ruby

Wanli reign of Ming Dynasty
Unearthed from the Dingling Mausoleum of the Ming Tombs in Changping District, Beijing
Length 11 cm, Width 2.4 cm
The Ming Tombs Museum

孝靖后首饰。顶部花形托上镶白玉鸳鸯，在鸳鸯腹部又嵌石榴子红宝石一块。

Jewelry of Empress Xiaojing. The flower-shaped holder at the top is inlaid with white jade mandarin duck, and a pomegranate ruby is embedded in the belly of the mandarin duck.

掐丝嵌珠宝花蝶金耳坠（一对）

明万历
北京市昌平区明十三陵定陵出土
高 5.5 厘米
明十三陵博物馆藏

Filigreed gold earring with butterflies and flowers design inlaid with gems (1 pair)

Wanli reign of Ming Dynasty

Unearthed from the Dingling Mausoleum of the Ming Tombs in Changping District, Beijing

Height 5.5 cm (each)

The Ming Tombs Museum

孝靖后首饰。

Jewelry of Empress Xiaojing.

花丝镶嵌

Filigree Inlay

掐丝是花丝工艺的基础技法
（出自《中国传统工艺全集·金银细金工艺和景泰蓝》）
Filigreeing is the basic technique of filigree craftsmanship
(Source: *Complete Collection of Traditional Chinese Crafts: Metal Filigree and Cloisonne*)

錾刻
（出自《中国传统工艺全集·金银细金工艺和景泰蓝》）
Carving
(Source: *Complete Collection of Traditional Chinese Crafts: Metal Filigree and Cloisonne*)

花丝镶嵌工艺又称细金工艺，为"花丝"和"镶嵌"两种制作技艺的结合。与景泰蓝、玉雕、雕漆等八大工艺门类，合称"燕京八绝"，充分汲取各地民间工艺的精华，开创了中国传统工艺的新高峰。花丝工艺是将金属用拔丝板拉成细丝后，再采用掐、填、攒、焊、编、织、堆、垒等技法塑造器物的造型。镶嵌工艺是以挫、锼、捶、闷、打、崩、挤、镶等技法，将金属片做成托或凹槽，使珍珠、宝石等固定在器物上作为装饰。明代中晚期，花丝镶嵌工艺以编织、堆垒技法见长，运用大量宝石，色泽明丽，气质华贵。

Filigree inlay technology is a kind of metalwork combining filigree and inlay. It is known as Beijing Eight Imperial Handicrafts together with cloisonne, jade carving, lacquer carving and others. By fully absorbing the essence of folk crafts from various regions, filigree inlay opened up a new peak of Chinese traditional crafts. Filigree technology is to shaping an object into different forms through a series of processes by making the precious metal into fine strands or wires, then pinching, filling, uniting, welding, plaiting and stacking. Inlaying is to make the metal plate into holders or grooves to fix pearls and gems on the objects as ornaments by rasping, carving, hammering, sealing, striking, breaking, squeezing and inlaying. During the mid and late Ming Dynasty, filigree inlay techniques were known for their plaiting and stacking techniques by applying a large number of gemstones to bring out the bright luster and luxurious temperament.

累丝嵌宝石花蝶金簪

明万历
北京市昌平区明十三陵定陵出土
长 27.3、宽 9.9 厘米
明十三陵博物馆藏

Filigreed gold hairpin with flowers and butterflies inlaid with gems

Wanli reign of Ming Dynasty
Unearthed from the Dingling Mausoleum of the Ming Tombs
in Changping District, Beijing
Length 27.3 cm, Width 9.9 cm
The Ming Tombs Museum

　　孝靖后首饰。下部为半圆弧形。顶为云头形累丝，上托花、蝶形花丝镶嵌。分为两部分，每部分又分为两层花样。一部分底托为葵花及花叶，上凸花蕊三个，每个中心嵌宝石一块（红宝石二块，蓝宝石一块），珍珠二颗，上层为一蝴蝶，蝶背部嵌蓝宝石一块，须部各系一珍珠。上下两层花在中心有插套相套合在一起。另外，在套外还焊接有贯形鼻两个，分别插入犀角及莲花花枝。另一部分下层为覆葵花托，上承葵花，上层为菊花，花蕊部分嵌红宝石一块，上下层花在中心也有插套相套合，在套外焊接有贯形耳四个，分别插入嵌有宝石的花枝及云形花，二者相间，共嵌宝石八块（红宝石、蓝宝石各四块）。

Jewelry of Empress Xiaojing. The lower part is in a semi-circular arc shape. The top is filigreed in a Ruyi-sceptre shape, which pops up filigreed and inlaid with flowers and butterflies into two parts. Each part is further divided into two layers of patterns. One part with the collet of sunflowers and leaves, with three protruding stamens on top. The center of each is embedded with one gemstone (two rubies and one sapphire), two pearls, and the upper layer is a butterfly. The back of the butterfly is embedded with a sapphire, and its whiskers are each adorned with a pearl. The upper and lower layers of flowers are plugged together in the center. In addition, two coin-shaped noses are welded outside the sockets, which are respectively inserted with rhinoceros' horns and lotus spray. The other part is affixed with a collet to hold the sunflower in the lower part, and chrysanthemums on the upper part, and the stamen is embedded with a ruby. The upper and lower layers of flowers are also plugged in the center, and there are four coin-shaped ears welded outside the sockets, which are inserted with sprays inlaid with gems and cloud-shaped flowers. The two are interphase, and are embedded with a total of eight gemstones (four rubies and four sapphires).

嵌红宝石仙人骑凤金簪

明万历
北京市昌平区明十三陵定陵出土
长 12.8、宽 3 厘米
明十三陵博物馆藏

Filigreed gold hairpin inlaid with ruby and an immortal riding phoenix

Wanli reign of Ming Dynasty

Unearthed from the Dingling Mausoleum of the Ming Tombs in Changping District, Beijing

Length 12.8 cm, Width 3 cm

The Ming Tombs Museum

孝靖后首饰。顶部为仙人骑凤，凤昂首展翅，每翅上嵌宝石一块。仙人为一老者，面部作嬉笑状，长髯，双手持如意，肩披斗篷，并有长长的飘带自肩部过两腋垂至下部。

Jewelry of Empress Xiaojing. The top is an immortal riding a phoenix with its head raised and wings spread. Each wing is inlaid with a gem. The immortal is an old man with a playful face and a long beard. He holds a Ruyi scepter in both hands and wears a cloak with long ribbons hanging from his shoulders to lower armpits.

制瓷工艺
Porcelain Making Craft

明朝中后期，民营手工业的发展远超官营手工业。以瓷器而言，代表晚明制瓷业水平的是全国制瓷中心——江西景德镇。景德镇瓷器产品占据了当时中国的主要市场，其民窑产品畅销中外，纹饰、题材、画意与官窑瓷器有着明显的区别，造型也有诸多创新。

During the mid and late Ming Dynasty, private handicrafts developed more vigorously than official handicrafts. In terms of porcelain, Jingdezhen, a national porcelain center in Jiangxi Province, represented the highest level of porcelain industry in the late Ming Dynasty. The products there occupied the main market in China at that time. Its folk kiln products sold well both at home and abroad. Their patterns, themes, and artistic conception were significantly different from those of the official kilns, and their modelings were also innovative.

青花梅瓶

明嘉靖
北京市昌平区明十三陵定陵出土
通高 46、口径 6.3、底径 12.2 厘米
明十三陵博物馆藏

Blue-and-white porcelain prunus vase

Jiajing reign of Ming Dynasty

Unearthed from the Dingling Mausoleum of the Ming Tombs
in Changping District, Beijing

Overall Height 46 cm, Mouth Diameter 6.3 cm,
Bottom Diameter 12.2 cm

The Ming Tombs Museum

小口微侈，束颈，广肩，瘦腹，平底。有覆碗形盖，盖顶有圆钮，下有一孔眼，盖内顶部有空心柱状体。白地青花，肩、腹部以双线为界将花纹分作四部分：上部饰倒垂状连续如意云头纹，云头内饰莲花纹，二云头之间饰璎珞纹；第二部分饰串枝番莲纹；第三部分为梅花纹；下部饰变形莲瓣纹。盖外壁饰云纹，顶饰八宝纹。肩部有"大明嘉靖年制"款。

定陵共出土青花梅瓶 8 件，6 件属万历时期，2 件属嘉靖时期。形制基本相同，仅大小和纹样有差异，为研究明代青花瓷的发展情况提供了难得的资料。

The vase has a small slightly flared mouth, a narrow neck, wide shoulders, a thin belly, and a flat bottom. It has a cover in the shape of an upturned bowl, and a rounded knob on the top with a hole below, and a hollow column at the top of the cover. The vase of blue patterns over white ground is divided into four parts with double rings on the shoulders and belly: The upper part is decorated with an inverted and continuous Ruyi-sceptre design, and lotus flower pattern is adorned in the Ruyi-sceptre, and in between, it is decorated with the design of tassels; the second part is decorated with the design of interlocking passionflowers and lotus branches; the third part is the plum blossom pattern; the lower part is decorated with a stylized lotus petal pattern. The outer wall of the cover is decorated with cloud design, and the top is decorated with the design of eight Buddhist emblems. There is the inscription "Made in the Jiajing reign of Great Ming" on the shoulder.

A total of 8 blue-and-white porcelain prunus vases were unearthed in the Dingling Mausoleum, of which 6 belonged to the Wanli reign and 2 the Jiajing reign. They share a similar shape and structure, with only differences in size and pattern, and are valuable materials for studying the development of blue-and-white porcelain in the Ming Dynasty.

青花花鸟纹碗

明万历
高 5.2、口径 9.1、底径 4.3 厘米
北京艺术博物馆藏

Blue-and-white porcelain bowl with flower and bird design

Wanli reign of Ming Dynasty
Height 5.2 cm, Mouth Diameter 9.1 cm,
Bottom Diameter 4.3 cm
Beijing Art Museum

景德镇窑制，为万历时期民窑常见瓷器品种。碗内素白，外壁饰青花图案。口沿和圈足各饰弦纹两圈。腹部饰兰草、洞石、折枝花果与飞鸟。绘画采用勾线平涂技法，具有鲜明的时代风格与特色。外底中心书青花仿"大明成化年制"六字双行单圈楷书款。

Made in Jingdezhen kiln, it was a common type of porcelain in folk kilns during the Wanli reign. The bowl is plain white inside, and is decorated with blue-and-white pattern on the outer wall. Two rings of bow-string design are decorated along the rim and ring foot. The belly is decorated with the design of orchids, cave stones, plucked branches, flowers and fruits, and flying birds. The painting adopts the technique of line drawing and flat color, with a distinct style and characteristics of the times. There is a blue-and-white inscription in the single ring in the center of the outer bottom imitating "Made in the Chenghua reign of Great Ming" in two lines of six Chinese characters in regular script.

青花人物纹盘

明万历
高 4、口径 23.4、底径 16.1 厘米
北京艺术博物馆藏

Blue-and-white porcelain plate with figure design

Wanli reign of Ming Dynasty
Height 4 cm, Mouth Diameter 23.4 cm,
Bottom Diameter 16.1 cm
Beijing Art Museum

景德镇窑制，为万历时期常见瓷器样式。胎质细腻，通体饰青花图案。外壁饰折枝花果纹，内壁饰一圈龙戏珠纹与云凤纹。内底饰"萧何月下追韩信"历史故事图：韩信立于江边待渡，周围衬托着柳树、船只及缭绕的云雾；萧何策马扬鞭从远方奔驰而来。构图巧妙，绘画精细。外底中心书青花"大明万历年制"双圈双行楷书款。

Made in Jingdezhen kiln, it was a common type of porcelain during the Wanli reign. The body texture is smooth and decorated with blue-and-white patterns all over. The outer wall is decorated with the design of plucked branches, flowers and fruits, while the inner wall is decorated with the design of a ring of dragons playing with a pearl and clouds, and phoenixes. The inner bottom is decorated with a picture of the historical story of "Xiao He Chasing Han Xin Under the Moon": Han Xin stands by the river waiting to cross, surrounded by willow trees, boats, and coiled-up clouds; Xiao He gallops on his horse with a whip in his hand from the distance. The composition is ingenious and the brushwork is meticulous. A blue-and-white inscription "Made in the Wanli reign of Great Ming" in the two-line regular script is marked in the double-ring in the center of the outer bottom.

青花莲托八宝纹盒

明万历
高 5.2、口径 19.3、底径 13.9 厘米
北京艺术博物馆藏

Blue-and-white porcelain box with the design of lotus and eight Buddhist emblems

Wanli reign of Ming Dynasty

Height 5.2 cm, Mouth Diameter 19.3 cm,
Bottom Diameter 13.9 cm

Beijing Art Museum

景德镇窑制。为万历时期官窑常见瓷器品种。胎体厚重，造型规整，器里素白，外壁饰青花图案。腹上部饰三角几何形图案，并于轮廓线内填绘花卉纹。腹下部饰缠枝莲托八宝纹。绘画采用勾线平涂技法，构图严谨，画工精细。外底中心书青花"大明万历年制"六字三行双圈楷书款。

Made in Jingdezhen kiln, it was a common type of porcelain in official kilns during the Wanli reign. The body is thick and well-shaped. The inner wall is plain white. The outer wall is decorated with blue-and-white design. The upper belly is adorned with triangular geometric patterns and filled with floral patterns inside the triangles. The lower part of the belly is adorned with the design of interlocking lotus flowers and branches as well as eight Buddhist emblems. The painting adopts the technique of line drawing and flat color, with rigorous composition and meticulous craftsmanship. A blue-and-white inscription "Made in the Wanli reign of Great Ming" of six Chinese characters in the three-line regular script is marked in the double rings in the center of the outer bottom.

青花龙穿花纹罐

明万历
高 5.8、口径 4.1、腹径 8.7、底径 6.1 厘米
北京艺术博物馆藏

Blue-and-white porcelain jar with the design of dragons amidst flowers

Wanli reign of Ming Dynasty
Height 5.8 cm, Mouth Diameter 4.1 cm,
Diameter of Belly 8.7 cm, Bottom Diameter 6.1 cm
Beijing Art Museum

　　景德镇窑制。造型小巧，胎质细腻，釉面肥厚莹润。器内施白釉，外壁饰青花图案。肩上饰覆莲瓣纹，腹部饰莲池游龙纹，胫部饰海水江崖纹，近底处饰仰莲瓣纹。画面层次清晰，青花艳丽深沉，色调蓝中泛紫。"龙穿花"为万历时期官窑瓷器常见装饰纹样。外底中心书青花"大明万历年制"六字三行双圈楷书款。

Made in Jingdezhen kiln, the jar is delicate in shape, fine and smooth in body texture and thick and translucent in glaze. The vessel is white glazed inside and decorated with blue-and-white design on the outer wall. The shoulder is adorned with inverted lotus-petal patterns, the belly is adorned with the design of dragon swimming in a lotus pond, the shin part is adorned with stylized waves and mountain peaks, and the near-bottom is decorated with upward lotus-petal patterns. The picture is distinctive in layers; the blue-and-white patterns are dignified, showing a purple hue in blue. The design of "dragons amidst flowers" was a common decorative pattern on official kiln porcelain during the Wanli reign. A blue-and-white inscription "Made in the Wanli reign of Great Ming" of six Chinese characters in three-line regular script is marked in the double rings in the center of the outer bottom.

青花云龙纹罐

明万历
高 50.7、口径 25.5、腹径 47.7、底径 27 厘米
北京艺术博物馆藏

Blue-and-white porcelain jar with the cloud and dragon design

Wanli reign of Ming Dynasty
Height 50.7 cm, Mouth Diameter 25.5 cm,
Belly Diameter 47.7cm, Bottom Diameter 27 cm
Beijing Art Museum

景德镇窑制。造型硕大，胎体厚重。器内施白釉，外壁通体饰青花图案。肩部饰缠枝花卉纹一周，腹部饰云龙纹和草书"寿"字，以草书字与纹饰结合表达吉祥寓意。近底处饰海水江崖纹。纹饰布局满密，青花发色浓艳。外底中心内凹，书青花"大明万历年制"六字双行双圈楷书款。是晚明时期官窑瓷器常见装饰方式。

Made in Jingdezhen kiln, the jar has a large shape with a thick and heavy body. The inner wall is white glazed, and the outer wall is decorated with blue-and-white patterns all over. The shoulder is adorned with a ring of interlocking flower patterns, while the belly is adorned with the cloud dragon design and the character "*Shou* (longevity)" in cursive script, which expresses auspicious meanings together with the decorative patterns. The design of stylized waves and mountain peaks is adorned near the bottom. The pattern layout is dense, and the blue-and-white design is rich and bright. The center of the outer bottom is concave, marked with a blue-and-white inscription "Made in the Wanli reign of Great Ming" of six Chinese characters in three-line regular script in double rings. It is a common decoration method for official kiln porcelain in the late Ming Dynasty.

背面
The Back

蓝釉碗

明万历
高 13.3、口径 30、底径 13 厘米
北京艺术博物馆藏

Blue glazed porcelain bowl

Wanli reign of Ming Dynasty

Height 13.3 cm, Mouth Diameter 30 cm,
Bottom Diameter 13 cm

Beijing Art Museum

　　景德镇窑制，为明代瓷器传统品种之一。胎壁厚薄适中，造型规整。内外通体施蓝釉，色调深沉，呈色稳定。口沿一圈因釉料垂流，色调浅淡，蓝中泛白。外腹部饰锥刻云龙纹，近底处饰锥刻仰莲瓣纹，锥刻技法娴熟，线条纤细，若隐若现。外底施白釉，中心暗刻"大明万历年制"六字双行双圈楷书款。

Made in Jingdezhen kiln, it was one of the traditional varieties of porcelain in the Ming Dynasty. The bowl is moderate in body wall thickness and regular in shape. The bowl is overall glazed blue in and out in a deep and stable hue. The color of the rim looks whitish blue due to the drooping of the glaze. The outer belly is needle carved with the cloud and dragon design, and the lotus petal pattern is taper-carved near the bottom. The taper-carved shows superb techniques, with slender lines that are faintly visible. The outer bottom is white glazed, and the center is incised with a double-ring blue-and-white inscription "Made in the Wanli reign of Great Ming" of six Chinese characters in the two-line regular script in double rings.

青釉花卉纹盘

明万历
高 6.8、口径 37.9、底径 16.5 厘米
北京艺术博物馆藏

Celado glazed porcelain plate with the flowers and plant design

Wanli reign of Ming Dynasty
Height 6.8 cm, Mouth Diameter 37.9 cm,
Bottom Diameter 16.5 cm
Beijing Art Museum

龙泉窑制。通体施青釉，釉面开冰裂纹。釉薄处色青泛白，釉厚处色青泛绿。盘外壁光素无纹，内壁饰刻划蕉叶纹，内底饰模印折枝花卉纹。外底中心内凹，局部施青釉，釉层较薄，可见旋坯痕。

Made in Longquan kiln, the object is overall glazed celadon, showing broken-ice crackles. The thin glazed area looks whitish green, while the thick glazed looks bluish green. The outer wall is plain with no design, while the inner wall is etched with the plantain-leaf design, and the inner bottom is pressed with the design of plucked branches of flowers. The center of the outer bottom is concave and partially coated with celadon glaze in a relatively thin glaze layer, with visible base spiraling marks.

彩瓷工艺
Painted Porcelain Craft

明代在宋、金、元彩瓷基础上进一步烧造出许多创新品种的彩瓷，如五彩、斗彩、素三彩，并发展了青花、蓝釉、红釉的制作工艺。明代匠人还将彩色装饰运用到绘画、镶嵌工艺和金银器制作中。明代的制瓷业空前繁荣，既有为朝廷烧造器物的官窑——御窑厂，更有遍地林立的民窑。到 16 世纪末，位于江西省鄱阳湖畔的景德镇成为世界瓷都，那里有数以万计的陶瓷工匠，他们制作的瓷器不仅供应国内市场，并且出口世界各地。

The Ming Dynasty made further progress in painted porcelain on the basis of the Song, Jin, and Yuan dynasties with many innovative varieties, such as polychrome, contending colors, and plain tricolor, and developed the production techniques of blue-and-white, blue glaze, and red glaze. The craftsmen also applied color decoration to painting, inlay techniques and metalworks. The porcelain industry in the Ming Dynasty boomed unprecedentedly, with not only the official kilns that fired artifacts for the court - the imperial kilns, but also numerous folk kilns. By the end of the 16th century, Jingdezhen, located on the banks of Poyang Lake in Jiangxi Province, became the world's porcelain capital, where tens of thousands of ceramic craftsmen engaged in the business. The products they made were not only demanded in the domestic market, but also exported to various parts of the world.

五彩梅花式盆

明万历
高 7.8、口径 30.4、底径 19.2 厘米
北京艺术博物馆藏

Polychrome plum-blossom-shaped porcelain basin

Wanli reign of Ming Dynasty
Height 7.8 cm, Mouth Diameter 30.4 cm,
Bottom Diameter 19.2 cm
Beijing Art Museum

景德镇窑制，为万历时期官窑瓷器样式。整体为五瓣梅花式，造型规整，胎质细腻，釉面莹润，通体饰青花五彩图案。口沿内饰锦地开光水藻与游虾，外饰落花流水纹。内外壁均采用通景式构图，分别饰水中游虾和江边芦雁。内底饰海水江崖、奔跑的双鹿、盛开的梅花、飞舞的双蝠及乾卦符号，象征福禄齐天。图案布局满密，色彩丰富艳丽。外底中心内凹，书青花"大明万历年制"六字双行双圈楷书款。

Made in Jingdezhen kiln, it is a common style of official kiln porcelain in the Wanli reign. The overall design is a five-petal-plum-blossom style, with a regular shape, delicate body texture, and a glossy glaze. The whole body is decorated with blue-and-white and polychrome patterns. The inner rim is adorned with algae and swimming shrimps over reserved panels, and the outer rim is adorned with the design of ripples. Both the inner and outer walls adopt a panorama-style composition, decorated with swimming shrimps in the water and wild geese by the river. The inner bottom is adorned with the design of stylized waves and mountain peaks, two running deers, blooming plum blossoms, two flying bats, and diagrams of the *Qian*, symbolizing boundless wealth and fortune. The pattern layout is dense and colorful. The center of the outsole is concave, marked in the double ring with a blue-and-white inscription "Made in the Wanli reign of Great Ming" of six Chinese characters in two-line regular script.

三彩花鸟人物瓷觚

明万历

北京市昌平区明十三陵定陵出土

高 25.6、口径 16、底径 12.5 厘米

明十三陵博物馆藏

Tri-color porcelain *Gu* with flowers, birds and figures designs

Wanli reign of Ming Dynasty

Unearthed from the Dingling Mausoleum of the Ming Tombs in Changping District, Beijing

Height 25.6 cm, Mouth Diameter 16 cm, Bottom Diameter 12.5 cm

The Ming Tombs Museum

出于万历皇帝梓室北侧。以黄、灰褐、黑三色釉绘彩。颈、腹及圈足两侧附有条状凸棱，仿铜觚。口内侧绘菊花纹，外侧颈部绘山石、花卉、蜂蝶、蜻蜓等草虫纹；肩部饰云头纹；腹部两侧绘有人物故事，上有流云，下有草地，松荫下一人骑马出行，马后紧跟二躬身侍者，近者持扇，远者捧书，表现出毕恭毕敬的姿态。马前一侧一人跪坐在地上，似在诉说着什么，身后绘有栅栏。另一侧，一人前跪而后顾，前面有牛一头，似在前跑又突然停下向后观望。圈足上部绘四季花卉纹，下部饰卷草纹。觚底有款："大明万历年制"。

Unearthed from the north side of Wanli Emperor's outer coffin, the vessel is painted with yellow, grayish brown, and black glazes. There are flanges on either side of the neck, belly, and ring foot, in imitation of copper *Gu* (wine vessel). The inner rim is painted with chrysanthemum patterns, while the outer neck is painted with designs of rocks, flowers, bees, butterflies, dragonflies, and so on; the shoulder part is decorated with Ruyi-sceptre design; a story is painted on either side of the belly, with flowing clouds above and grass below. Under the shade of pine, a man rides a horse and is followed by two bowing attendants closely behind. The nearer one is holding a fan and the farther one is holding a book, looking respectful. A person in front of the horse sits on the ground in a kneeling position, as if talking about something, with a fence painted behind him. On the other side, a man looks back on his knees, with a cow in front, seems to run forward, and suddenly stops to look back. The upper part of the ring foot is decorated with seasonal flower patterns, and the lower part is decorated with floral scrolls. At the bottom of the *Gu*, it is marked: "Made in the Wanli reign of Great Ming".

Exchange Between China and the West

晚明是中国古代社会转型的重要阶段。这一时期城市化进程加快，国内外市场进一步扩大，商品经济空前繁荣，海内外文化交流频繁。从思想观念到社会风俗，从文学艺术到百工技艺，无不蓬勃发展，蕴含着巨大的文化趣味和精神魅力，中国文化艺术的发展进入了重要的历史时期。大航海时代的交通贸易不仅让海外的物质文明进入中国，也使中外思想文化相互交融。

The late Ming Dynasty was an important stage of social transformation in ancient China, with accelerated urbanization, further expansion of domestic and international markets, an unprecedented flourishing commodity economy, and frequent cultural exchanges between the East and West. The Chinese culture and art ushered an important historical period of thriving development, from ideological concepts to social customs, from literature and arts to craftsmanship, presenting enormous cultural interest and spiritual charm. The transportation and trade during the Age of Discovery not only introduced overseas material civilization into China, but also promoted the integration of Chinese and foreign ideologies and cultures.

第三单元

外融
中交

《清明上河图》卷是明代画家仇英创作的一幅风俗画作品。此画整体参照了张择端《清明上河图》的构图布局，即从郊外到虹桥、城门、城内大街，再到城外的顺序。不同的是，张择端描绘的是北宋时期汴京的市井风貌，而仇英画作所表现的是明代中期苏州的社会生活图景。画中人物共两千多个，且神态各异，栩栩如生。整卷内容十分丰富，涵盖了经济、文化、科技等方方面面，是研究明代中后期社会生活和文化的重要图证。

The Riverside Scene at Qingming Festival is a genre painting created by Ming Dynasty painter Qiu Ying. It basically referred to the overall composition layout of Zhang Zeduan's Riverside Scene at Qingming Festival, which goes from the suburbs to the Rainbow Bridge, the city gate, the main streets inside the city, and then to the outside the city. The difference is that Zhang Zeduan depicts the urban landscape of Bianjing during the Northern Song Dynasty, while Qiu Ying's painting represents the social life of Suzhou in the mid Ming Dynasty. There are over two thousand figures in the painting, each with a different expression, very lifelike. The entire scroll is very rich in content, covering economy, culture, technology and various other aspects. It is an important graphic material for studying the social life and culture of the middle to late Ming Dynasty.

《清明上河图卷》（局部）（明）仇英　辽宁省博物馆藏
The Riverside Scene at Qingming Festival (detail) by Qiu Ying (Ming)　Collection of the Liaoning Provincial Museum

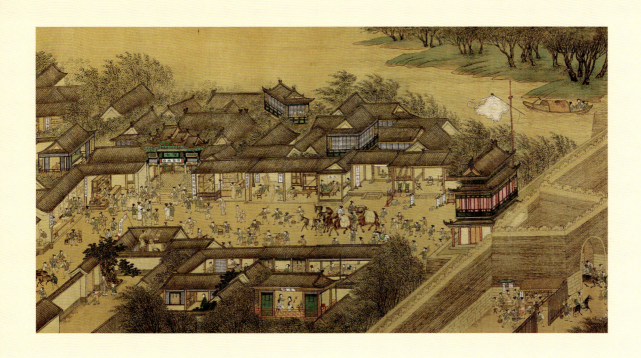

明代赋税

Taxation of the Ming Dynasty

明代赋税有本色、折色之称，以米、麦交纳称本色，而将税粮折成金、银、钞、钱、绢、布、漆等交纳，谓之折色。正统时，明廷把江南的田赋折成银两，解入内承运库，专供宫廷之用，称为"金花银"。万历六年（1578年）强令加金花银二十万两，每年达一百二十万两。定陵出土银锭铭文记录了所解府、州、县名及年代和重量，甚至记录了知州、知县和银匠的姓名。为研究明代后期经济发展情况、赋税制度提供了材料。

The taxation in the Ming Dynasty was divided into "*Bense*（本色）" and "*Zhese*（折色）". The former refers to the tax paid on rice and wheat, while the latter means the tax paid on gold, silver, paper money, silver, silk, cloth, lacquer converted from the grain tax. During the Zhengtong reign, the Ming court converted the land tax in regions south of the Yangtze River into silver taels and transferred them to the national treasury exclusively for the court use, known as "*Jinhuayin* (gold floral silver)". In the sixth year of Wanli reign (1578), two hundred thousand taels of gold floral silver were imperatively added, reaching 1.2 million taels per year. The inscriptions on silver ingots unearthed from the Dingling Mausoleum recorded the names of the prefectures, states districts as well as the date and weight they sent to the court, even the names of the prefects, the magistrates and silversmiths, which provide valuable materials for studying the economic development and tax system in the late Ming Dynasty.

"万历通宝"铜钱 (2枚)

明万历
北京市昌平区明十三陵定陵出土
直径 2.5、方穿 0.5 厘米
明十三陵博物馆藏

"Wanli Tongbao" copper coin (2 pcs)

Wanli reign of Ming Dynasty

Unearthed from the Dingling Mausoleum of the Ming Tombs
in Changping District, Beijing

Diameter 2.5 cm, Diameter of Square Hole 0.5 cm

The Ming Tombs Museum

　　圆形，边缘上有郭。正方形穿，穿之两面有内郭。正面有阳文"万历通宝"。万历通宝始铸于万历四年（1576年）。万历中后期，因战争、营建帝陵等巨大支出，为应对日益困窘的财政状况，明朝廷铸钱数量大增，且质量不高，致使钱价骤跌、通货膨胀。

Round coin with a raised rim, square hole in the center, which also has raised rim on both the observe and the reserve. The observe is carved with "Wanli Tongbao" in relief. Wanli Tongbao was first minted in the fourth year of Wanli reign (1576). In the mid to late Wanli reign, the Ming court increased the mintage immensely, usually in low quality, in response to the increasingly difficult financial situation due to huge expenditures in wars and the construction of imperial mausoleums, which lead to a sharp drop in the value of money and inflation.

正面
The Front

正面
The Front

背面
The Back

背面
The Back

金饼

明万历
北京市昌平区明十三陵定陵出土
长2.4、宽2、厚0.2~0.5厘米
明十三陵博物馆藏

Gold

Wanli reign of Ming Dynasty

Unearthed from the Dingling Mausoleum of the Ming Tombs
in Changping District, Beijing

Length 2.4 cm, Width 2 cm, Thickness 0.2-0.5 cm

The Ming Tombs Museum

桃形，尖部较薄，下部较厚。

Peach-shaped cake, with a thinner tip and thicker lower part.

金饼

金锭

明万历
北京市昌平区明十三陵定陵出土
长 6.2、腰宽 2.8、厚 1.5 厘米
明十三陵博物馆藏

Gold ingot

Wanli reign of Ming Dynasty

Unearthed from the Dingling Mausoleum of the Ming Tombs
in Changping District, Beijing

Length 6.2 cm, Width of Waist 2.8 cm, Thickness 1.5 cm

The Ming Tombs Museum

亚腰形，正面中部微凹，背面稍鼓。正面刻"九
成色金十两"，背面刻"万历四十六年户部进到大兴
县铺户严洪等买完"。

Narrow-waisted ingot, slightly concave in the middle of the front
side, slightly bulging on the back. The obverse is engraved with
"ten taels of 90% gold content", and the reverse is engraved with
"In the 46th year of the Wanli reign, the Ministry of Revenue came
to Daxing District and bought all from Yan Hong and others shop
owners".

明万历

北京市昌平区明十三陵定陵出土

长 5.1、腰宽 2、厚 1.4 厘米

明十三陵博物馆藏

Gold ingot

Wanli reign of Ming Dynasty

Unearthed from the Dingling Mausoleum of the Ming Tombs
in Changping District, Beijing

Length 5.1 cm, Width of Waist 2 cm, Thickness 1.4 cm

The Ming Tombs Museum

亚腰形，两端上翘较高，正面中部微凹，有水波纹，
背面呈弧形。

Narrow-waisted ingot, with both ends raised high, slightly concave
in the middle of the front side, with water ripple design, and arc-
shaped back.

金锭

明万历

北京市昌平区明十三陵定陵出土

长 5.6、腰宽 2.6、厚 1.6 厘米

明十三陵博物馆藏

Gold ingot

Wanli reign of Ming Dynasty

Unearthed from the Dingling Mausoleum of the Ming Tombs in Changping District, Beijing

Length 5.6 cm, Width of Waist 2.6 cm, Thickness 1.6 cm

The Ming Tombs Museum

亚腰形，正面中部微凹，两端上翘呈弧形，背面平。底刻"云南布政司计解万历三十六年分足色金壹锭重拾两委官通判张荐金户余汝贵金匠沈教"。

定陵共出土 103 枚金锭，其中 79 锭出自万历帝棺内，21 锭出自孝端后棺内，另外 3 锭分别出自帝后椁内棺顶东端。金锭有大小两种，大的十两，上面都镌刻铭文或粘贴纸标签。从铭文可知，金锭主要来自云南和顺天府的大兴、宛平二县，这与文献记载相符。云南本不产金，云南当地政府不得不向四川、贵州等地购买。

Narrow-waisted ingot, slightly concave in the middle of the front side, with both ends raised in arc shape, and flat back side. The bottom is inscribed with 37 Chinese characters describing the date, the gold content, the goldsmith, and other information.

A total of 103 gold ingots were unearthed from the Dingling Mausoleum, of which 79 ingots were from Wanli Emperor's coffin, 21 from Emperor Xiaoduan's coffin, and the other 3 ingots from the eastern end of the top of the inner coffins of the emperor and the empress. Gold ingots come in two sizes, the larger being ten taels, with inscriptions carved or paper labels tagged on them. From the inscriptions, it can be seen that the gold ingots mainly came from Yunnan Prefecture, and Daxing and Wanping districts of Shuntian Prefecture, which is consistent with literature records. Gold was not produced in Yunnan, and the local government had to purchase it from Sichuan, Guizhou, and other places.

银锭

明万历

北京市昌平区明十三陵定陵出土

长7.6、腰宽3.5、厚1.8厘米

明十三陵博物馆藏

Silver ingot

Wanli reign of Ming Dynasty

Unearthed from the Dingling Mausoleum of the Ming Tombs
in Changping District, Beijing

Length 7.6 cm, Width of Waist 3.5 cm, Thickness 1.8 cm

The Ming Tombs Museum

亚腰形，正面中心稍凹，两端呈弧形凸起，背面稍平。正面刻"银作局花银拾两"。

Narrow-waisted ingot, slightly concave in the center of the front side, with raised edges in an arc shape at both ends, and slightly flat back. The obverse is engraved with "ten taels of gold floral silver of Silverwork Bureau".

银锭

明万历

北京市昌平区明十三陵定陵出土

长 11.7、腰宽 4.2、厚 2.5 厘米

明十三陵博物馆藏

Silver ingot

Wanli reign of Ming Dynasty

Unearthed from the Dingling Mausoleum of the Ming Tombs
in Changping District, Beijing

Length 11.7 cm, Width of Waist 4.2 cm, Thickness 2.5 cm

The Ming Tombs Museum

亚腰形，正面中心稍凹，两端呈弧形凸起，背面稍平。正面刻"银作局花银叁拾两"。

Narrow-waisted ingot, slightly concave in the center of the front
side, with raised edges in an arc shape at both ends, and slightly
flat back. The obverse is engraved with "thirty taels of gold floral
silver of Silverwork Bureau".

银锭

明万历
北京市昌平区明十三陵定陵出土
长 10.2、腰宽 4.8、厚 2 厘米
明十三陵博物馆藏

Silver ingot

Wanli reign of Ming Dynasty

Unearthed from the Dingling Mausoleum of the Ming Tombs
in Changping District, Beijing

Length 10.2 cm, Width of Waist 4.8 cm, Thickness 2 cm

The Ming Tombs Museum

正面刻"银作局花银贰拾两"。

银锭是明代主要的流通货币，定陵共出土 65 锭，分别出自万历帝和孝端、孝靖皇后的棺椁内，有五十两、三十两、二十两和十两四种。银锭主要来自江西、浙江各府、州、县。从铭文来看，有京库银、米银、折银、金花银等。金花银专供宫廷所需。

The obverse is engraved with "Twenty taels of gold floral silver of Silverwork Bureau".

Silver ingots were the main circulating currency of the Ming Dynasty. A total of 65 silver ingots were unearthed from the Dingling Mausoleum, which were respectively from the coffins of Wanli Emperor, Empress Xiaoduan, and Empress Xiaojing. They come in fifty, thirty, twenty, and ten taels. The silver ingots mainly came from various prefectures, states, and districts in Jiangxi and Zhejiang. From the inscriptions of ingots, they include *Jingkuyin*, *Miyin*, *Zheyin*, and *Jinhuayin*, etc. *Jinhuayin* was exclusively for court use.

一 百花齐放

I. Booming Literature, Arts and Science

明代后期，随着农业、手工业、商品经济的迅速发展，文化发展呈现出传承与创新兼备的风格。印刷术的进步和刻书业的发展，为文化传播创造了良好的条件。戏曲、小说、诗集以及画谱大量出现，各种日用类书广泛传播，蔚为大观，影响深远。在此背景下，明代后期的文化、科技成绩斐然。

The cultural development presented a style combining inheritance and innovation in the late Ming Dynasty with the rapid development of agriculture, handicrafts, and commodity economy. The progress of printing and the development of the block-print industry created favorable conditions for cultural dissemination. Drama, novels, poetry anthologies, and pictorial books emerged like the spring of mushrooms. Various books for everyday use were widely spread, creating a magnificent and far-reaching impact. In this context, the late Ming Dynasty made brilliant achievements in culture and technology.

小说创作

Novel Creation

　　明代的小说创作十分兴盛，产生了大量以历史、神怪及市民日常生活为题材的长篇章回体小说。成书于元末明初的《三国演义》《水浒传》和成书于明中叶的《西游记》，标志着中国古典长篇小说的成熟。明中叶以后，随着宋元话本的整理刊行，文人摹拟宋元话本而创作拟话本之风日盛，短篇白话小说大量出现，如冯梦龙辑纂的《喻世明言》《警世通言》《醒世恒言》，收入宋、元、明话本及拟话本一百二十篇，反映出当时市民阶层的思想、生活和情趣，对后世的白话小说及戏曲都有很大影响。

The creation of novels gained momentum in the Ming Dynasty, resulting in a large number of full-length chapter-style novels themed with history, gods and spirits, and the daily lives of citizens. *Romance of the Three Kingdoms* and *Water Margin* written in the late Yuan and early Ming dynasties, and *Journey to the West* written in the mid-Ming dynasty, marked the maturity of Chinese classical novels. After the mid Ming Dynasty, with the collation and publication of the scripts of storytelling of Song and Yuan dynasties, the creation of novels written in the style of scripts of storytelling prevailed, and a large number of short vernacular stories appeared, such as *Stories to Instruct the World, Stories to Caution the World*, and *Stories to Awaken the World* compiled by Feng Menglong, which included 120 scripts of storytelling of the Song, Yuan, and Ming dynasties. They reflected the thoughts, lives, and tastes of the common people at that time, and had a great impact on later vernacular novels and operas.

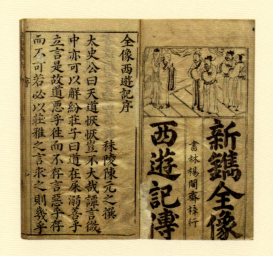

《鼎镌京本全像西游记》

（明）　吴承恩撰　明杨闽斋刻本

Full Length Edition of Journey to the West by Wu Cheng'en (Ming, *Dingjuan Jingben*), Yang Minzhai block-printed edition in the Ming Dynasty

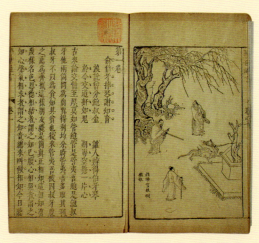

《警世通言》

（明）　冯梦龙撰　明金陵兼善堂刻本

Stories to Caution the World by Feng Menglong (Ming), Jinling Jianshantang block-printed edition in the Ming Dynasty

戏曲
Opera

　　明朝在我国戏曲史上是继元代杂剧之后的第二个黄金时代，戏剧成为城市居民不可缺少的文化活动。明代中后期，随着城镇经济的繁荣，戏曲又出现了新的发展，产生了许多具有进步意义的作品，如汤显祖的代表作《牡丹亭》等。

The Ming Dynasty was the second golden age in the history of traditional Chinese opera, following the *Zaju* of Yuan Dynasty, and opera became an indispensable cultural activity for urban residents. In the mid to late Ming Dynasty, with the prosperity of the urban economy, traditional Chinese opera underwent new developments with the appearance of many progressive works, such as Tang Xianzu's representative work *Peony Pavilion*.

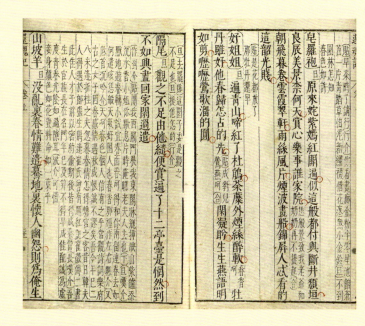

《牡丹亭》

（明）汤显祖撰　明末怀德堂刻本

Peony Pavilion by Tang Xianzu (Ming), Huaidetang block-printed edition in the late Ming Dynasty

画谱
Pictorial Books

　　万历时期是中国版画史上的黄金时代，形成了以南京、徽州、杭州为代表的数个版画刻印中心。这一时期产生的版画作品数量也十分可观，几乎占据了版画全史的半壁江山。坊间为了教学，刊印了大量带有专题性质的画谱，《唐诗画谱》《宋词画谱》均为其中的精品之作。

The Wanli reign was a golden age in the history of Chinese printmaking, formed with several printmaking centers represented by those in Nanjing, Huizhou, and Hangzhou. The number of printmaking works produced during this period was also very considerable, accounting for almost half of the history of printmaking. A large number of pictorial books with special topics for teaching were published in the bookshops, among which the *Pictorial Book of Tang Poetry* and *Pictorial Book of Song Ci-pomes* were among the quality works.

《唐诗画谱》

（明）　黄凤池撰　明万历集雅斋刻本

Pictorial Book of Tang Poetry compiled by Huang Fengchi (Ming), Jiyazhai block-printed edition of Wanli reign of Ming Dynasty

日用类书

Reference Books for Daily Use

万历时期，日用类书流通广泛。日用类书是相对于官修大型类书及文人学者私撰类书而言的、由书坊编刊而成的一类书籍，主要供百姓日常实用、道德教育及文化娱乐之需要。其书将日常生活所需之各种常识，例如农桑、医药、饮食、居室、穿戴、路程、车乘、历法、气象、刑律、赋税、算术、命相、劝善、救济、蒙养、尺牍等，分门别类汇于一编，或摘录典籍，或采自民俗，或出以俚语，或图文并茂，以提供士农工商随时便用为宗旨，如同今日俗称之家庭生活手册。

Reference books for daily use were widely circulated during the Wanli reign. Compared to large government-compiled books and private books written by literati and scholars, they were a type of books compiled and published by bookstores, to meet the needs of daily life, moral education, and cultural entertainment of the common people. The book categorizes various common knowledge needed for daily life, such as agriculture, medicine, diet, living quarters, clothing, journey, transportation, calendar, meteorology, criminal law, taxation, arithmetic, divination, ethics, relief, moral education, and letter writing in one. The content either excerpts from ancient books, extracts from folk customs, cites from slang, or combines pictures and essays are both excellent, with the aim of providing convenient use for scholars, farmers, artisans, and merchants, just like today's family life manual.

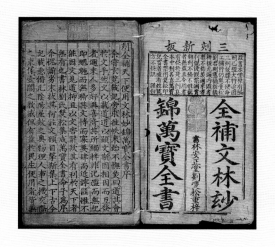

《新板全补天下便用文林妙锦万宝全书》

（明）　刘双松编

明万历四十年（1612 年）安正堂刻本

Complete Encyclopedia for Everyday Life Use with New Supplement compiled by Liu Shuangsong (Ming), Anzhengtang block-printed edition in the 40th year of the Wanli reign of Ming Dynasty (1612)

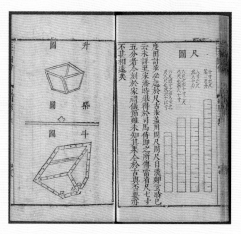

《三才图会》

（明）　王圻、王思义撰

明万历三十七年（1609 年）原刊本

Illustration of the Three Powers by Wang Qi and Wang Siyi (Ming), the original issue in the 37th year of the Wanli reign of the Ming Dynasty (1609)

科学著作
Scientific Works

在经济繁荣和生产实践的推动下，明代科学技术也得到了长足发展，产生了一批享誉世界的作品。这些著作在总结历代科技成果的基础上多有发明和创新，把中国科学技术推进到新的水平，同时对世界科技文明产生了积极影响。

Driven by economic prosperity and production practices, science and technology in the Ming Dynasty also made significant progress and created a number of world-renowned works. These works have made many inventions and innovations on the basis of summarizing the scientific and technological achievements of previous dynasties, pushing China's science and technology to a new level, also exerting a positive impact on the world's scientific and technological civilization.

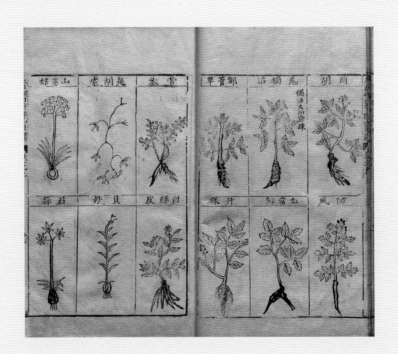

《本草纲目》

（明）李时珍撰　明万历二十四年（1596 年）金陵胡承龙刻本

Compendium of Materia Medica by Li Shizhen (Ming), Jinling Hu Chenglong block-printed edition in the 24th year of the Wanli reign of the Ming Dynasty (1596)

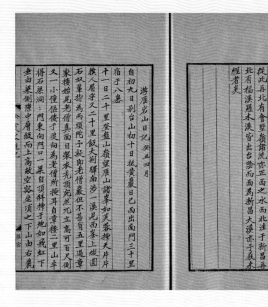

《农政全书》

（明）　徐光启撰　明崇祯十二年（1639 年）陈子龙平露堂刻本

The Encyclopedia on Agricultural Administration by Xu Guangqi (Ming), Chen Zilong Pinglutang block-printed edition in the 12th year of the Chongzhen reign of the Ming Dynasty (1639)

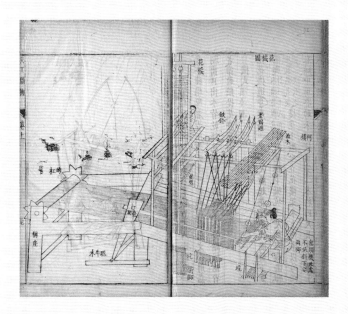

《天工开物》

（明）　宋应星撰　明崇祯十年（1637 年）宋应星自刻本

The Exploitation of the Works of Nature by Song Yingxing (Ming), the block-printed edition of Song Yingxing himself in the tenth year of the Chongzhen reign of the Ming Dynasty (1637)

书画艺术
Calligraphy and Painting Art

明代后期，社会变革、个性解放，雅俗界限变得模糊，社会风气渐从质朴向浮华转变，人们开始追求奢华享乐。很多书画家创作出大量风格鲜明、率真任性的作品，流派纷呈、风格各异而且成就较高，形成浪漫、洒脱、个性、变革的晚明书画独特风格。

The boundary between elegance and vulgarity became blurred in the late Ming Dynasty with the social transformation and individual liberation, and the general mood of the society gradually shifted from simple to flashy. People began to pursue luxuries and comforts. A large number of works with distinct and straightforward styles were created by calligraphers and painters, with diverse genres and high attainments, forming a unique style of late Ming calligraphy and painting that was romantic, free and easy, personalized, and transformative.

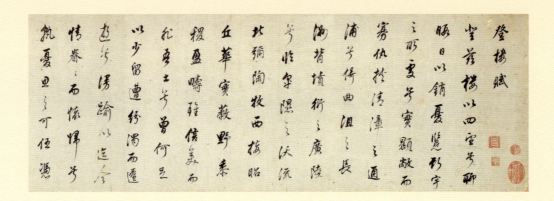

《登楼赋》（局部）（明）董其昌

辽宁省博物馆藏

Poetry of Climbing the Tower (detail) by Dong Qichang (Ming)
Collection of Liaoning Provincial Museum

《仿仇英人物山水长卷》（局部）（明）佚名

杭州市临平博物馆藏

Copy of *Long Scroll Painting of Landscape and Human Figures by Qiu Ying* (detail), Anonymous (Ming)
Collection of Linping Museum in Hangzhou

张宏 幽溪渔隐图轴

明万历
画心纵 128.2、横 56.3 厘米
北京艺术博物馆藏

Scroll painting of *Hermit Fisherman in a Remote Stream* by Zhang Hong

Wanli reign of Ming Dynasty
Painting: Length 128.2 cm, Width 56.3 cm
Beijing Art Museum

这是一件明代画家张宏所绘的水墨设色山水立轴。画面上远山近崖、江水蜿蜒，江岸绿柳垂荫，崖上苍松巨树，林木屋宇掩映其间，近处一人执桨荡舟欲穿峡而过。画面题款："幽溪渔隐，辛卯新秋写于昆陵寓次，吴门张宏"。后钤白文印二方："张宏""君度氏"。另有鹤涧老人重题诗一首。

This is a vertical scroll of colored landscape painting in ink and wash painted by the Ming Dynasty painter Zhang Hong (1577-1652). In the picture, there are two mountains, one far and the other near, and a winding river; the riverbank is shaded by green willows, and the mountains are covered by towering pine trees, with trees and houses hidden amidst them; a fisherman is paddling a boat to cross the gorge in the foreground. The inscription on the painting: "Hermit fisherman in a remote stream, created in the early autumn of Xinmao (1591) at Kunling studio, Zhang Hong of the Wu school." Followed by two stamped seals in white legend: "Zhang Hong" and Jundu (his courtesy name) and another poem by Hejian (his literary name).

吴治 小山招隐图轴

明万历
画心纵 183、横 46.5 厘米
北京艺术博物馆藏

Scroll painting of *Hermit in the Mountains* by Wu Zhi

Wanli reign of Ming Dynasty
Painting: Length 183 cm, Width 46.5 cm
Beijing Art Museum

　　此作品为明代画家吴治所绘《小山招隐图》，水墨设色绢本立轴。画面山势巍峨，云气弥漫中有奇石异树、亭台楼阁，在画家营造的如仙境般的场景中，有隐士生活其中。画面题跋："遁迹淮南兮世绪昌，桂树丛生兮连崇冈。小山嵯峨兮多伏藏，栋宇连云兮翠幌张。牙签插架兮书能香，猿鹤成群兮谿渚傍。秫田堪酿兮厨琼浆，逍遥玩世兮多醉乡。八公邂逅兮遗丹方，甲子初週兮鬓未苍。鸿宝著成兮能翱翔，啸咏荪枝兮日月长。师之社兄六秩初度，令弟希之。兄索手绘小山招隐图以祝之，涂完系以一歌为侑觞之叹。峨眉逸人吴治画并题。"题头钤印三方：朱文"延陵"，白文"画印""志在山水"，题尾钤印两方，朱文"吴治之印"，白文"淮南小隐"。

Hermit in the Mountains is a silk scroll ink and wash painting with colors created by the Ming Dynasty painter Wu Zhi. In the picture, the mountains are towering, with grotesque rocks and rare trees, pavilions, and towers amidst the dense clouds. A hermit can be seen in the landscape like a fairyland created by the painter. In the remarks of the scroll, the painter depicts the beautiful scenery in the mountains and narrates that he created the painting to celebrate his friend's 60th birthday upon his request. In the front of the inscription, it is stamped with three seals: "Yanling" in red legend, "*Huayin* (painting seal)" and "Aspiration in Mountains and Rivers" in white legend. At the end of it, it is stamped with two seals: "Seal of Wu Zhi" in red legend, and "Huainan Hermit" in white legend.

方大猷 山水图轴

明万历
画心纵 187、 横 51 厘米
北京艺术博物馆藏

Scroll painting *Landscape* by Fang Dayou

Wanli reign of Ming Dynasty
Painting: Length 187 cm, Width 51 cm
Beijing Art Museum

　　此作品为明代画家方大猷所绘水墨山水，绫本立
轴。画面上山势耸立，山瀑流泉，山林掩映屋宇。近
处屋中两人据案对坐，携一童子观瀑。中近屋宇中两
人倚栏俯观流泉，远景林屋渐隐于云气之中。画面题
款"壬寅芒种日似天器，杨老亲翁世壶，方大猷"。
后钤白文印两方："方大猷印""允升氏"。

It is a vertical scroll ink landscape on satin by the Ming Dynasty
painter Fang Dayou. In the picture, there are towering mountains,
waterfalls and flowing springs, with houses hidden in the mountains
and forests. In the foreground, two people sit opposite each other
watching the waterfall with a boy. In the middle ground, two people
lean against the railing and look down at the flowing stream. In the
background, the houses gradually fade into the forest and clouds.
There is an inscription on the painting, with two seals at its end:
"Seal of Fang Dayou" and "Yunsheng (his literary name)".

刘原起 山水扇面

明万历
画心纵 16.5、横 51 厘米
北京艺术博物馆藏

Fan face *Landscape* by Liu Yuanqi

Wanli reign of Ming Dynasty
Painting: Length 16.5 cm, Width 51 cm
Beijing Art Museum

This is a fan leaf freehand painting of ink on gold paper with color by the Ming Dynasty painter Liu Yuanqi. The picture depicts the scenery of a mountain dwelling by the water, with a pavilion on the mountain, a temple on the bank in the middle ground, and endless distant mountains in the background. The brushwork is rather unrestrained with a blend of ink and color in a distinctive gradient, full of elegant taste. The inscription reads: "In the 2nd month of Xinyou Tianqi, Yuanqi". Followed with a stamped seal, "Liu Zhenzhi". On the left side, it is stamped with a gourd-shaped seal "Shi Gong", and a rectangle seal "Fuli Zhao Zhuo Zhenwan" in red legend.

Liu Yuanqi (?-?) originally named Zuo, known for his courtesy name, courtesy name "Zi Zheng" and "Zhenzhi", was an important painter of the Wu School in the Ming Dynasty. As a disciple of Qian Gu, he got the hang of his master's spirit and exceled in painting landscapes, flowers, and writing poetry.

　　此作品为明代画家刘原起所绘金笺扇面，水墨设色小写意。画面描绘水边山居之景，山上有亭，中景岸边有寺庙，远山连绵不绝。用笔较疏放，墨色交融，层次分明，颇富有文人雅趣。款署"天启辛酉二月写，原起。"后钤白文印一方"刘氏振之"。左侧另钤葫芦形朱文印一方"石公"，长方形朱文印一方"甫里赵卓珍玩"。

　　刘原起（生卒年不详），初名祚，以字行，更字子正、振之。为明代吴门画派重要画家，师钱榖，颇肖其神，善画山水、花卉，工诗。

倪元璐 行书轴

明万历
画心纵 112、横 37 厘米
北京艺术博物馆藏

Scroll of calligraphy in running script by Ni Yuanlu

Wanli reign of Ming Dynasty
Painting: Length 112 cm, Width 37 cm
Beijing Art Museum

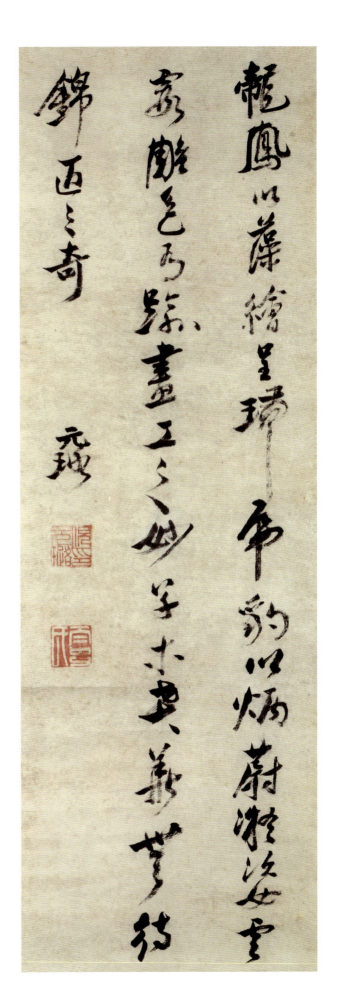

　　这是明代书家倪元璐的行书作品，纸本立轴。用笔苍古劲爽，行中带草，结字跌宕奇逸，章法字距茂密，行距宽疏，注重节奏变化，书法以气骨见长。其书深得颜鲁公厚实劲健之笔意，而更为劲峭，结体趋于扁方，呈敧侧之势，以险寓正，风格奇倔刚毅，于明末自成一格。款署"元璐"，后钤印两方，朱文"倪元璐印"及白文"太史氏"。

　　倪元璐（1593～1644 年），浙江上虞人。天启二年（1622 年）进士，历官至户、礼两部尚书。李自成入京时，自缢死，福王谥其号"文正"。其书、画俱佳。

This is a vertical scroll of calligraphy in running script on paper by the Ming Dynasty calligrapher Ni Yuanlu. The brushwork looks primitive and robust, with dense characters and sparse lining space with a sense of cursive running script to emphasize the change of rhythm. His calligraphy is known for its momentum and strength and bearing the calligraphic style of Yan Lugong (Yan Zhenqing), yet even more vigorous. The structure tends to be flat and square, leaning to a side to imply upright with steep strokes, showing an exceptionally stubborn and resolute style. He had formed a style of his own in the late Ming Dynasty. The scroll is with the inscription of "Yuan Lu", followed by two stamped seals: "Seal of Ni Yuanlu" in red legend and "Taishi" in white legend.

Ni Yuanlu (1593-1644), born in Shangyu, Zhejiang, became *jinshi* in the second year of Tianqi (1622). He served as the Minister of Revenue and the Minister of Rites successively. When Li Zicheng attacked Beijing, he hanged himself and was posthumously named "Wenzheng" by Prince Fu. He was celebrated both for his calligraphy and paintings.

陈继儒 书法册

明万历
画心纵 21、横 14 ～ 16 厘米
北京艺术博物馆藏

Calligraphy sheet by Chen Jiru

Wanli reign of Ming Dynasty
Painting: Length 21 cm, Width 14-16 cm
Beijing Art Museum

此幅作品为明代书画家陈继儒所书，纸本册页。书法行中带草，笔意在苏轼、米芾之间，意态生动、流畅自然，看似随意，实则法度严谨，颇具古意。款署"陈继儒"，后钤印两方，白文"陈继儒印"及朱文"眉公"。另有鉴藏印五方。原签条题"陈眉公字册真迹"。

陈继儒（1558 ～ 1639 年），明代文学家、书画家，与同郡董其昌齐名。字仲醇，号眉公、麋公。华亭（今上海松江）人。诸生，屡被荐举，坚辞不就。工诗文、书画，书法师法苏轼、米芾，书风萧散秀雅。擅墨梅、山水，作品多册页小幅。

This is a calligraphy sheet on paper by Chen Jiru, a calligrapher and painter of the Ming Dynasty. The work in running cursive script bears the calligraphic styles of Su Shi and Mi Fu, looking vivid, smooth, and natural. The strokes appear to be casual, but are actually rigorous and elaborate in order, full of antique interests. The work is with the inscription of "Chen Jiru", followed by two stamped seals: "Seal of Chen Jiru" in white legend and "Meigong" in red legend. There are also five stamped seals of appreciation and collection. The original tag reads "Authentic copy of Chen Meigong's calligraphy".

Chen Jiru (1558 - 1639), courtesy name Zhongchun, literary name Meigong, Migong, born in Huating (today's Songjiang, Shanghai), was a writer, calligrapher, and painter of the Ming Dynasty, equally famous with Dong Qichang of the same prefecture. He was an imperial scholar (*Xiucai*), but declined to be an official after having been repeatedly recommended. He excelled in poetry and writing, calligraphy and painting. Inheriting the calligraphic styles of Su Shi and Mi Fu, his calligraphy is unrestrained and elegant. He was proficient in plum blossoms and landscape painting in ink, and most of his works are small-sized calligraphy sheets.

5 | 6

7 | 8

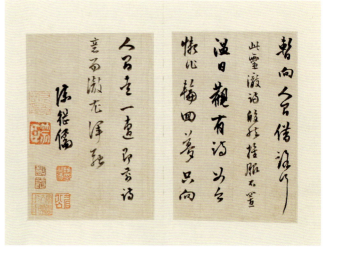

文房场景

Scene of Scholar's Room

　　唐以后，文人的书房雅称"文房"。文房是文人读书习作、燕闲清赏、雅集畅叙之所。明人文房家具造型简雅朴素，随着书画艺术的发展与兴盛，书房陈设器具也日臻完备，这些既是文人精神世界的外化体现，亦是中国传统文化的重要载体。

After the Tang Dynasty, the study of literati was given a good name "Wenfang (scholar's room)". It is where the literati read and write, enjoy leisure and appreciate art, and meet and chat with friends. The furniture in the study of the Ming Dynasty was simple and elegant in modelling. With the development and thriving of calligraphy and painting art, the furnishings and utensils in the study also became ample and refined, which were not only the externalized manifestations of the literatis' spiritual world, but also important carriers of traditional Chinese culture.

黄花梨独心板平头案

明
长 199、宽 55、高 79 厘米
恭王府博物馆藏

Huanghuali single-plank flat-ended table

Ming Dynasty
Length 199 cm, Width 55 cm, Height 79 cm
Princ Kung's Palace Museum

通体黄花梨制，案面长条形，攒框镶板心，边抹冰盘沿线脚。面下装素牙板、牙头，前后牙板末端封以牙堵。圆材直腿，腿足侧脚收分明显，前后腿间装两根圆材梯枨。

此种平头案早在两宋时期即已定型，明代广为流行，为明式家具的典型样式。

Made of Huanghuali wood, the table has a long narrow top with an apron set with the panel and extended beading along the edge. A plain apron board and apron-head spandrel are affixed to the top. The ends of the front and back apron are sealed with bastion. Straight legs in roundwood, with obvious contracture at the side foot of the legs. Two roundwood ladder braces are set between the front and back legs.

The plane-ends narrow table was fashioned as early as the Northern and Southern Song Dynasties and was well-received in the Ming Dynasty, forming a typical style of Ming furniture.

黄花梨夹头榫小翘头案

明
长 92.2、宽 42.2、高 76.8 厘米
恭王府博物馆藏

Huanghuali wood long table with up-turned ends

Ming Dynasty
Length 92.2 cm, Width 42.2 cm, Height 76.8 cm
Princ Kung's Palace Museum

通体黄花梨制小翘头案。面下装有素牙板、云纹牙头，前后牙板末端封以牙堵，劈料做圆材直腿，牙板与腿夹头榫相交。截面呈瓜棱形，腿足侧脚收分明显。前后腿间装两根方材梯枨。小翘头案翼然灵动，瓜棱腿别致隽美，整体造型清秀雅致。

This is a small Huanghuali table with upturned ends. Beneath the surface, it features a plain serrated board and a cloud-patterned apron-head spandrel. The ends of the front and back aprons are capped with serrated plugs, while the legs are made of roundwood split from the same material, intersecting with the apron via elongated bridle joints. The cross-section of the legs exhibits a melon-ridged shape, with the side feet displaying a noticeable tapering effect. Between the front and back legs, two square ladder braces are installed, adding stability to the overall structure. The small table with upturned ends exudes a graceful and delicate elegance. Its winged ends lend a lively and agile quality, while the melon-ridged legs are exquisitely unique and charming.

黄花梨四出头官帽椅 (1 对)

清
长 65、宽 58、高 117 厘米
恭王府博物馆藏

Huanghuali wood official's hat-shaped chair with four protruding ends (1 pair)

Qing Dynasty
Length 65 cm, Width 58 cm, Height 117 cm
Prince Kung's Palace Museum

通体黄花梨制对椅，搭脑中部呈枕式，两端弯曲向后上翘出头，扶手弯曲外撇出头，俗称四出头官帽椅。靠背板三段攒成，依次饰透雕螭纹、浮雕梅花山石、鱼门洞及亮脚。鹅脖与前腿、靠背立柱与后腿均一木连坐。座面下装浮雕卷草纹壶门式券口牙板，两侧装洼堂肚式券口牙板。足底四根管脚枨，前面的一根最低，两侧两根次之，最后一根最高，为"步步高赶枨"，寓意步步高升。

此对四出头官帽椅用材考究，体形硕大，可供人结跏趺坐，故又称为"禅椅"。

The chair made of Huanghuali wood comes in pair. The backrest is in a style of pillow in the middle, with its ends warped backward, the handrail bends and flares out of the head, commonly known as official's hat-shaped chair with four protruding ends. The backrest board is made of three sections, decorated with hollow carved dragon design, plum and stone design, fish-shaped hole and a "brightening-the-feet" opening in relief. The armrest posts and the front legs, the backrest posts and the hind legs are in one piece connected to the seat. The aprons of the seat are embossed with decorative patterns. For the four braces at the feet, the front one is the lowest, the two on the right and left sides are a little higher, and the hind one is the highest. That was "rising higher step by step", which means step by step to rise high.

This pair of official's hat-shaped chair with four protruding ends is particular about the material used and has a large seat, which allows one to sit cross-legged, so it is also called "chair for meditation".

黄花梨雕螭纹圈椅（一对）

清
长 60、宽 46、高 97 厘米
恭王府博物馆藏

**Huanghuali wood round-backed armchair
(1 pair)**

Qing Dynasty
Length 60 cm, Width 46 cm, Height 97 cm
Princ Kung's Palace Museum

通体黄花梨制对椅，造型典雅匀称，线条柔曲舒展，是明式圈椅中的精品。五接弧形椅圈，自搭脑伸向两侧，通过后边柱顺势而下，形成扶手。靠背板稍向后弯曲，形成背倾角，坐感舒适。靠背板两侧角牙，与靠背板一木连做，上雕一窠浮雕螭纹开光，形象生动，刀法快利。四角立柱与腿一木连做，"S"形联帮棍。席心座面，座面下装壶门券口，起边线。四腿外撇，侧脚收分，意在增加椅子的稳定性。腿间管脚枨自前向后逐步升高，称"步步高赶枨"，寓意步步高升。

This pair of chairs, crafted entirely from Huanghuali wood, exudes elegance and symmetry with its gracefully curved lines, making it a fine example of Ming-style round-backed armchairs. The five-jointed arc-shaped chair rail extends gracefully from the headrest to both sides, descending smoothly through the rear pillars to form the armrests. The backrest panel is subtly curved backwards to create a comfortable leaning angle. The two corner ornaments on the sides of the backrest panel are carved from the same piece of wood, featuring a lively and intricate relief carving of intertwined dragon motifs. The four corner posts and legs are also crafted from a single piece of wood, incorporating an "S"-shaped connecting brace.

The seat is made of woven cane, with an apron and arched frame underneath. The legs are flared outward, with the side feet tapering inwards, enhancing the chair's stability. The horizontal stretchers between the legs rise gradually from front to back, a design known as "ascending step by step," which symbolizes continuous progress and advancement in one's career.

二 交流互鉴

II. Exchange and Mutual Learning

明初郑和七下西洋，大规模的海上远航与探险延续了宋元以来海上丝绸之路的辉煌。隆庆元年（1567年），朝廷调整海外贸易政策，允许远贩东西二洋，使得民间海外贸易获得合法地位。明朝后期，手工业生产持续发展，工商业市镇迅速崛起，欧亚各地商人前来中国贸易，大量白银涌入中国，商品经济和白银货币经济达到前所未有的高度，明朝经济社会呈现出全新的开放局面。

In the early Ming Dynasty, Zheng He made seven voyages to the West. The oceangoing voyages in big fleets continued the glory of the Maritime Silk Road since the Song and Yuan dynasties. In the first year of Longqing reign (1567), the court adjusted its overseas trade policy, allowing the sale of goods overseas, and legitimating private foreign trade. In the late Ming Dynasty, handicraft production continued to develop, and industrial and commercial towns emerged one after another. Merchants from various regions of Europe and Asia came to China to do business, and a large amount of silver flooded into China. The commodity economy and silver currency economy reached unprecedented heights, and the Ming Dynasty opened up its economy and society on an unseen scale.

瓷器外销
Porcelain Export

《水果，玻璃器皿和万历瓷碗静物写生》(1659 年)
威廉·卡尔夫
纽约大都会博物馆藏
Still Life with Fruit, Glassware and a Wanli Bowl (1659)
Willem Kalf
Collection of the Metropolitan Museum of Art

　　自万历中期始，中国与南洋、西方各国的瓷器贸易进入新的阶段。随着海外市场的开放，中国瓷器被葡萄牙、荷兰的商船源源不断地运往世界各地，受到欧洲社会的追捧与争相收藏。与此同时，欧洲流行的器物造型、纹样也被西方商人介绍到中国，以使景德镇生产的日用瓷更符合欧洲人的习惯。

From the mid-Wanli reign, the porcelain trade between China and Southeast Asian and Western countries entered a new stage. With the opening of overseas markets, Chinaware was continuously shipped by Portuguese and Dutch merchants to various parts of the world, and was well received by European society for appreciation and collection. At the same time, the shapes and patterns of artifacts popular in Europe were also introduced to China by Western merchants to make the daily porcelain produced in Jingdezhen more adaptable to European customs.

"南澳一号"沉船瓷器

Porcelain from the Shipwreck of Nan'ao Ⅰ

"南澳一号"明代沉船发现于2007年，位于广东省汕头市南澳岛东南三点金海域，是一艘明代晚期的外贸商船。沉船出水了大量珍贵文物，其中大多为明代东南沿海地区民窑生产的青花瓷器。这些瓷器不仅是明代科技与工艺的代表，也是海上丝绸之路文化与贸易交流的重要物证。

"Nan'ao Ⅰ", a shipwreck of the Ming Dynasty, was discovered in the three-pointed gold area southeast of the Nan'ao Island in Shantou City, Guangdong Province in 2007. A large number of precious cultural relics were salvaged from the shipwreck, and most of which were blue-and-white porcelain wares produced by folk kilns in the southeastern coastal areas of the Ming Dynasty. These porcelain pieces are not only representatives of Ming Dynasty technology and craftsmanship, but also important physical evidence of cultural and trade exchanges along the Maritime Silk Road.

"南澳一号"沉船实测图

Measured drawing of Nan'ao Ⅰ

青花海螺云龙纹碗

明

广东汕头"南澳一号"沉船遗址出水

高 9、口径 18.6、足径 7 厘米

国家文物局考古研究中心藏

Blue-and-white porcelain bowl with conch, cloud and dragon design

Ming Dynasty

Excavations of Nan' ao I Shipwreck in Shantou, Guangdong Province

Height 9 cm, Mouth Diameter 18.6 cm, Foot Diameter 7 cm

National Centre for Archaeology

景德镇窑制。胎体轻薄，胎巴曰，质细密，外底修坯跳刀痕明显。内外均施白釉，釉色泛青，足沿无釉处泛黄褐涩。以青花为饰，晕散效果明显，外壁绘青花地留白云龙纹，以双线勾勒花枝，内壁口沿下饰一周青花纹条带，内底心双圈内绘青花地海螺纹。外底心书青花窗格状方款。

Made in Jingdezhen kiln, the bowl has a thin and white body with a fine texture. The outer bottom has obvious trimming marks of the cutter. White glaze is applied both inside and outside, with a pale green glaze color and a yellowish brown on the unglazed areas along the ring foot. The white and blue decoration shows an obvious spreading effect at the edge. The outer wall is painted with blue ground, spaced with the white cloud and dragon design, and outlined with the design of flower branches in double lines. The rim of the inner wall is decorated with a band of blue-and-white design, and the inner bottom center is painted with blue-and-white conch design in the double rings. A blue-and-white inscription is marked in the lattice window-like square at the center of the outer bottom.

青花仕女纹盘

明
广东汕头"南澳一号"沉船遗址出水
高 7、口径 26、足径 12.4 厘米
国家文物局考古研究中心藏

Blue-and-white porcelain plate decorated with a lady

Ming Dynasty
Excavations of Nan'ao I Shipwreck in Shantou, Guangdong Province
Height 7 cm, Mouth Diameter 26 cm, Foot Diameter 12.4 cm
National Centre for Archaeology

漳州窑制。胎体厚重，胎色灰白，质较粗。以青花为饰，外壁口沿下绘两道弦纹，腹近底端绘一周弦纹，内壁腹部绘四朵折枝花卉纹，内底心绘仕女纹。

Made in Zhangzhou kiln, the plate has a thick and heavy body with grayish white color and a coarse texture, decorated with blue patterns. The rim of the outer wall is painted with two lines of bowstring pattern. A ring of bow-string pattern is decorated near the bottom of the belly. The design of four plucked branches of flowers is painted on the inner wall of the belly, and a lady motif is painted at the center of the inner bottom.

青花缠枝牡丹五彩花卉纹碗

明
广东汕头"南澳一号"沉船遗址出水
高 6.2、口径 12.1、足径 4.5 厘米
国家文物局考古研究中心藏

Blue-and-white porcelain bowl with interlocking branches of peony and polychrome design

Ming Dynasty

Excavations of Nan' ao I Shipwreck in Shantou, Guangdong Province

Height 6.2 cm, Mouth Diameter 12.1 cm, Foot Diameter 4.5 cm

National Centre for Archaeology

景德镇窑制。

Made in Jingdezhen kiln.

青花缠枝花卉葡萄纹碗

明

广东汕头"南澳一号"沉船遗址出水

高 9.6、口径 18.8、足径 7.5 厘米

国家文物局考古研究中心藏

Blue-and-white porcelain bowl with design of interlocking branches and flowers and grapes

Ming Dynasty

Excavations of Nan' ao I Shipwreck in Shantou, Guangdong Province

Height 9.6 cm, Mouth Diameter 18.8 cm, Foot Diameter 7.5 cm

National Centre for Archaeology

景德镇窑制。胎体轻薄，胎巴白，质细密。内外均施白釉，釉面光洁莹润。青花为饰，外壁绘缠枝花卉纹，以双线勾勒花枝。内壁绘四组葡萄纹，枝蔓缠连。内底心双圈内绘四片花叶纹，外底心书青花"万福攸同"四字双圈款。

Made in Jingdezhen kiln, the bowl has a thin and white body with a fine texture. The bowl is white glazed in and out with blue and patterns, looking smooth and bright. The outer wall is decorated with interlocking branches and flowers, with the sprays outlined in double lines. Four sets of grape designs are painted on the inner wall, with interlocking vines. Four floral and leaf patterns are painted in the double ring at the center of the inner bottom, while at the center of the outer bottom, it is marked with blue-and-white *"Wan Fu You Tong"* four characters in double rings.

青花缠枝花卉葡萄纹碗

青花人物纹碗

明

广东汕头"南澳一号"沉船遗址出水

高 5.9、口径 12.2、足径 4.8 厘米

国家文物局考古研究中心藏

Blue-and-white porcelain bowl with figure design

Ming Dynasty

Excavations of Nan'ao I Shipwreck in Shantou, Guangdong Province

Height 5.9 cm, Mouth Diameter 12.2 cm, Foot Diameter 4.8 cm

National Centre for Archaeology

景德镇窑制。胎体轻薄，胎色白，质细密。内外均施白釉，釉面光洁莹润。青花为饰，外壁绘二组骑马人物纹。内底心双圈内绘"高官厚禄"图，外底心书青花窗格状方款。

Made in Jingdezhen kiln, the bowl has a thin and white body with a fine texture. The bowl is white glazed in and out with blue-and-white patterns, looking smooth and bright. The outer wall is painted with the motif of two sets of horse-riding men. In the center of the inner bottom, it is painted with the motif of "high officials and good salaries" in a double ring. A blue-and-white inscription is marked in the lattice window-like square at the center of the outer bottom.

青花缠枝花卉纹玉壶春瓶

明
广东汕头"南澳一号"沉船遗址出水
高 14.8、口径 5.6、足径 5.5 厘米
国家文物局考古研究中心藏

Blue-and-white pear-shaped porcelain vase with flared lip and design of interlocking branches of peony

Ming Dynasty
Excavations of Nan'ao I Shipwreck in Shantou, Guangdong Province
Height 14.8 cm, Mouth Diameter 5.6 cm,
Foot Diameter 5.5 cm
National Centre for Archaeology

漳州窑制。胎体厚重，胎色灰白，质较粗。以青花为饰，外壁上、下以四道双弦纹作间隔，绘缠枝牡丹纹。

Made in Zhangzhou kiln, the vase has a thin and white body with a coarse texture and blue-and-white patterns. The outer wall is separated by four double-bowstring designs up and down, and painted with interlocking branches of peony.

青花缠枝花卉纹罐

明
广东汕头"南澳一号"沉船遗址出水
高 8、口径 4.3、底径 5.6 厘米
国家文物局考古研究中心藏

Blue-and-white porcelain jar with design of interlocking branches and flowers

Ming Dynasty

Excavations of Nan'ao I Shipwreck in Shantou,
Guangdong Province

Height 8 cm, Mouth Diameter 4.3 cm,

Bottom Diameter 5.6 cm

National Centre for Archaeology

漳州窑制。胎体厚重，胎色灰白，质较粗。以青花为饰，肩部、腹部绘缠枝花卉纹。

Made in Zhangzhou kiln, the jar has a heavy and grayish-white body with s coarse texture and blue-and-white patterns. The shoulder and belly are painted with interlocking branches and flowers.

青花牡丹纹菊瓣盒

明
广东汕头"南澳一号"沉船遗址出水
通高 7.8、口径 10.8、足径 6.4 厘米
国家文物局考古研究中心藏

Blue-and-white chrysanthemum-petal porcelain box with design of interlocking branches of peony

Ming Dynasty

Excavations of Nan' ao I Shipwreck in Shantou, Guangdong Province

Overall Height 7.8 cm, Mouth Diameter 10.8 cm, Bottom Diameter 6.4 cm

National Centre for Archaeology

景德镇窑制。盒身、盖可扣合，胎色白，质地细腻。外壁以青花为饰，身、盖口部均绘三角状条带，其内留白呈花瓣状纹，盖面双圈内绘团枝牡丹纹，外底心书有"福"字方框款。

Made in Jingdezhen kiln, the box has a white body of fine texture. The cover and the body can fit it. The outer wall is decorated with blue-and-white patterns, and the rims of the body and cover are painted with triangular stripes, with the space inside showing petal-shaped design. On the top of the cover, it is painted with interlocking branches of peony in a double ring. An inscription of the character "*Fu* (blessing)" is marked in a square box in the center of the outer bottom.

青花缠枝牡丹纹"福"款杯

明
广东汕头"南澳一号"沉船遗址出水
高4.2、口径6.6、足径2.4厘米
国家文物局考古研究中心藏

Blue-and-white porcelain cup with interlocking branches of peony design and an character of "*Fu* (blessing)"

Ming Dynasty

Excavations of Nan'ao I Shipwreck in Shantou, Guangdong Province

Height 4.2 cm, Mouth Diameter 6.6 cm,

Bottom Diameter 2.4 cm

National Centre for Archaeology

景德镇窑制。器形小巧，胎白质细。内外均青花纹饰，施白釉，釉面光洁莹润。外壁绘缠枝牡丹纹，外底心书"福"字款。

Made in Jingdezhen kiln, the cup has a delicate shape and white body of fine texture. Blue-and-white patterns are decorated in and out. The cup is white-glazed with smooth and bright luster. The outer wall is painted with the design of interlocking branches of peony. And at the center of the outer bottom, it is inscribed with the character "*Fu* (blessing)".

传教士来华

Missionaries in China during the Ming Dynasty

利玛窦与徐光启
Matteo Ricci and Xu Guangqi

　　明朝后期，意大利人利玛窦、石方西、郭居静、熊三拔、龙华民，葡萄牙人麦安东、孟三德、费奇规、罗如望、李玛诺，西班牙人庞迪我等来华传教。这些传教士在中国传播西方天文、数学、地理等科学技术知识，其见闻也被记录下来传回西方，重塑了西方人对中国的认识，从而实现了中西方在历史上的一次跨文化交流。

In the late Ming Dynasty, Matteo Ricci, Francois de Petris, Lazzaro Cattaneo, Sabbatino de Ursis, and Niccolo Longobardi from Italy, Antonio de Almeida, Edouard de Sande, Gaspar Ferreira, Jean de Rocha, and Emmanuel Diaz Senior from Portugal, and Diego de Pantoja from Spain came to China as missionaries. They spread Western scientific and technological knowledge including astronomy, mathematics, and geography in China, and recorded what they heard and saw and transmitted back to the West, where people gained a new understanding of China, thus achieving a cross-cultural exchange between China and the West in history.

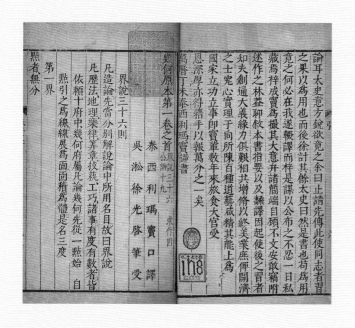

《几何原本》

(意大利)利玛窦口译、(明)徐光启笔受

明万历三十五年(1607年)初刻本

Euclid's Elements

Oral interpretation by Matteo Ricci (Italian) and written by Xu Guangqi (Ming)

The block-printed edition in the early 35th year of the Wanli reign of the Ming Dynasty (1607)

《几何原本》是我国最早的汉译西方数学专著之一。古希腊欧几里得撰写,意大利人利玛窦口述,明徐光启笔译,与《同文算指》同为当时研习数学知识、掌握西方算法的必读本。

Euclid's Elements is one of the earliest Western mathematical monographs translated into Chinese in China. The book was written by Euclid in ancient Greece, orally interpreted by Matteo Ricci, and translated by Xu Guangqi. The book and *Epitome of Arithmetic Practice* were considered required reading books for studying mathematical knowledge and mastering Western arithmetic at that time.

尾
声

1620 年，延续四十八年的万历时代落下帷幕，大明王朝的覆亡也依稀可见。

万历朝是一个充满矛盾与无奈的时代，当时中国所呈现的社会图景也是错综复杂的。在商品经济的冲击下，人们个性活跃、思想开放，文学创作兴盛蓬勃，艺术探索自由大胆。社会对于物质享受的热衷，推动了手工业的进步与商贸繁荣，于是山海宝藏骈集，器具珍玩各异，社会生活异彩纷呈。

与此同时，海禁重开、贸易再兴，海上丝绸之路的延续让东、西两个世界联系频繁。西方的知识技术传入中国，明朝的器物与文化也远播海外。东方与西方文明在早期全球化进程中遥相辉映、交流互鉴，推动着古代中国走向近代化。

In 1620, the Wanli reign, which had lasted for 48 years, came to an end, foreshadowing the fall of the Ming Dynasty.

The Wanli reign was an era full of contradictions and helplessness, and the time when the social landscape in China presented its complexity. Under the impact of the commodity economy, people pursued individuality with an open mind, literary creation thrived, and artistic exploration tended to be free and audacious. The social craving for material pleasure promoted the progress of handicrafts and the prosperity of commerce. As a result, social life became diversified and colorful with various treasures from mountains and sea gathered and different utensils and artifacts appeared.

At the same time, contact between the East and West became more frequent with the lifting of the ban on maritime trade, the revival of trade, and the continuation of the Maritime Silk Road. Western knowledge and technology were introduced to China, and the artifacts and culture of the Ming Dynasty were also spread overseas. The Eastern and Western civilizations shone on each other in distance through exchange and mutual learning, promoting ancient China to move towards modernity.

万历朝大事记

Milestones of the Wanli Reign

隆庆六年（1572 年）

◆ 五月，穆宗驾崩，以高拱、张居正、高仪三人为顾命辅臣。

◆ 六月，神宗朱翊钧即位；张居正任内阁首辅。

◆ 七月，尊穆宗皇后为仁圣皇太后，尊神宗生母李贵妃为慈圣皇太后。

万历元年（1573 年）

◆ 十一月，张居正上疏请行"考成法"。

◆ 是年建立新安县，县址在今深圳南头，取"革故鼎新，去危为安"之义。

万历三年（1575 年）

◆ 七月，戚继光主持的长城修缮工程竣工。

万历六年（1578 年）

◆ 二月，神宗大婚，娶孝端皇后王氏。

万历十年（1582 年）

◆ 六月，张居正去世。

◆ 八月，恭妃王氏生皇长子朱常洛。

万历十一年（1583 年）

◆ 神宗四度亲往天寿山察看陵址，最后卜定大峪山下的"吉壤"。

万历十二年（1584 年）

◆ 十一月，定陵开始营建。

万历十五年（1587 年）

◆ 西班牙舰队出征英国。

In the 6th year of Longqing (1572)

◆ In the fifth month, Emperor Muzong died and appointed Gao Gong, Zhang Juzheng, and Gao Yi as regents in his imperial posthumous edict.

◆ In the sixth month, Emperor Shenzong Zhu Yijun ascended the throne; Zhang Juzheng was appointed the Senior Grand Secretary of the Grand Secretariat.

◆ In the seventh month, Empress Muzong was honored as Empress Dowager Rensheng, and Noble Consort Li, the biological mother of Emperor Shenzong, was honored as Empress Dowager Cisheng.

In the 1st year of Wanli (1573)

◆ In the eleventh month, Zhang Juzheng submitted a memorial to the throne to implement "performance evaluations for officials".

◆ Xin'an District was established in the same year, with its location in today's Nantou, Shenzhen, to imply "destroying the old and establishing the new (*Xin*), and turning peril to safety (*An*)".

In the 3rd year of Wanli (1575)

◆ In the seventh month, the Great Wall restoration project supervised by Qi Jiguang was completed.

In the 6th year of Wanli (1578)

◆ In the second month, Emperor Shenzong married Empress Xiaoduan, of the Wang clan.

In the 10th year of Wanli (1582)

◆ In the sixth month, Zhang Juzheng died.

◆ In the eighth month, Princess Gong, of the Wang clan gave birth to the first son of the emperor, Zhu Changluo.

In the 11th year of Wanli (1583)

◆ Shenzong personally went to Tianshou Mountain four times to inspect the tomb site, and finally determined the "*Jirang* (graveyard with good *fengshui*)" at the foot of Dayu Mountain.

In the 12th year of Wanli (1584)

◆ In the eleventh month, the construction of the Dingling Mausoleum broke ground.

In the 15th year of Wanli (1587)

◆ The Spanish Armada invaded England.

万历朝大事记

Milestones of the Wanli Reign

万历朝大事记

Milestones of the Wanli Reign

万历十七年（1589 年）

◆ 是年始，神宗不视朝。

万历十八年（1590 年）

◆ 六月，定陵完工。

万历二十年（1592 年）

◆ 二月，蒙古部落首领哱拜纠合其子承恩、义子哱云及土文秀等叛乱，宁夏之役爆发。同年九月平定，是为"万历三大征"之一。

◆ 四月，日军侵入朝鲜，朝鲜向宗主国明朝求援，援朝抗倭战争开始，至万历二十六年结束，是为"万历三大征"之二。

万历二十二年（1594 年）

◆ 神宗以宦官为矿监税使，在全国范围内开矿榷税。

万历二十七年 (1599 年）

◆ 播州土司杨应龙叛乱，播州之役爆发，次年平定，是为"万历三大征"之三。

◆ 十月，册立皇长子朱常洛为太子。

万历三十三年 (1605 年）

◆ 熹宗朱由校出生。

万历三十四年 (1606 年）

◆ 恭妃王氏晋封皇贵妃。

万历三十八年 (1610 年）

◆ 十二月，思宗朱由检出生。

In the 17th year of Wanli (1589)

◆ From the beginning of the year, Emperor Shenzong refused to attend morning meetings.

In the 18th year of Wanli (1590)

◆ In the sixth month, the Dingling Mausoleum was completed.

In the 20th year of Wanli (1592)

◆ In the second month, the leader of the Mongolian tribe, Bobai, colluded with his son Cheng'en, his foster sons Boyun and Tu Wenxiu to rebel. The Battle of Ningxia broke out. In the ninth month of the same year, the rebellion was pacified, marking the first of the "Three Great Conquests of Wanli".

◆ In the fourth month, the Japanese army invaded Korea. Korea requested reinforcement from its suzerain Ming Dynasty. The war to resist Japanese aggression and aid Korea began, which ended in the 26th year of Wanli, marking the second of the "Three Great Conquests of Wanli".

In the 22nd year of Wanli (1594)

◆ Emperor Shenzong appointed eunuchs as mining supervisors and tax commissioners, and opened mines and collected taxes countrywide.

In the 27th year of Wanli (1599)

◆ Yang Yinglong, the chieftain of Bozhou, rebelled, and the Battle of Bozhou broke out. The following year, the rebels were defeated, marking the third of the "Three Great Conquests of Wanli".

◆ In the tenth month, Zhu Changluo, the eldest son of the emperor, was conferred the crown prince.

In the 33rd year of Wanli (1605)

◆ Emperor Xizong Zhu Youjiao was born.

In the 34th year of Wanli (1606)

◆ Princess Gong, the clan of Wang, was conferred the Imperial Noble Consort.

In the 38th year of Wanli (1610)

◆ In the twelfth month, Emperor Sizong Zhu Youjian was born.

万历朝大事记

Milestones of the Wanli Reign

万历三十九年（1611 年）

◆ 九月，皇贵妃王氏去世（天启年间追封孝靖皇太后）。

◆ 东林党争起。

万历四十二年（1614 年）

◆ 二月，慈圣皇太后李氏去世。

万历四十三年（1615 年）

◆ 男子张差持棍闯入太子居所慈庆宫，事涉郑贵妃，神宗不愿深究，将张差处死，是为明末三大案之"梃击案"。

万历四十四年（1616 年）

◆ 努尔哈赤建立后金政权。

万历四十六年 (1618 年）

◆ 努尔哈赤起兵反明，攻陷抚顺。明廷加派辽饷。

万历四十七年（1619 年）

◆ 明朝与后金在萨尔浒（今辽宁抚顺东大伙房水库附近）附近交战，萨尔浒之战是明清兴亡史上一次具有决定性意义的战争。

万历四十八年（1620 年）

◆ 四月，孝端皇后王氏去世。

◆ 七月，神宗病逝。

◆ 八月，光宗朱常洛即位，登基不久即病重。鸿胪寺丞李可灼进献红丸，自称仙丹，光宗服后去世，是为明末三大案之"红丸案"。

◆ 九月，熹宗朱由校即位。光宗宠妃李选侍尚居乾清宫，群臣为防其干预朝事，上疏请移居哕鸾宫，是为明末三大案之"移宫案"。

◆ 十月，神宗葬于定陵。

In the 39th year of Wanli (1611)

◆ In the ninth month, the Imperial Noble Consort Wang died (posthumously honored Empress Dowager Xiaojing during the Tianqi reign).

◆ The start of the Donglin factionalism.

In the 42nd year of Wanli (1614)

◆ In the second month, Empress Dowager Cisheng Li died.

In the 43rd year of Wanli (1615)

◆ A man named Zhang Chai, armed with a wooden staff, broke into the Ciqing Palace where the Crown Prince resided. Emperor Shenzong executed Zhang Chai and hushed the case up as it involved his Noble Consort Zheng. It was known as the "Case of the Wooden Staff Assault", one of the three major cases in the late Ming Dynasty.

In the 44th year of Wanli (1616)

◆ Nurhaci established the Later Jin regime.

In the 46th year of Wanli (1618)

◆ Nurhaci rose army against the Ming Dynasty and took down Fushun. The Ming court increased the Ming soldier's pay and provisions in Liaoning.

In the 47th year of Wanli (1619)

◆ The Ming Dynasty and the Later Jin fought in the vicinity of Sarhu (near the present-day Dahuofang Reservoir east of Fushun, Liaoning Province). The Battle of Sarhu was a decisive war in the history of the rise and fall of the Ming and Qing dynasties.

In the 48th year of Wanli (1620)

◆ In the fourth month, Empress Xiaoduan Wang died.

◆ In the seventh month, Emperor Shenzong died of illness.

◆ In the eighth month, Emperor Guangzong Zhu Changluo ascended the throne and soon became seriously ill. Li Kezhuo, a secretary of the Court of State Ceremonials, presented red pills and claimed to be magic pills. Emperor Guangzong died after taking the red pills. This was the "Red Pill Case", one of the three major cases of the late Ming Dynasty.

◆ In the ninth month, Emperor Xizong Zhu Youjiao was enthroned. Li Xuanshi, the favored consort of Emperor Guangzong, was still living in the Palace of Heavenly Purity. The ministers submitted memorials to relocate her to the Palace of Phoenix lest she would interfere in the court affairs. It was the "Palace Relocating Case", one of the three major cases of the late Ming Dynasty.

◆ In the tenth month, Emperor Shenzong was buried in the Dingling Mausoleum.

万历朝大事记

Milestones of the Wanli Reign

图书在版编目（CIP）数据

万历那些年 ：万历文物主题特展 ：汉英对照／深
圳市南山博物馆编 ． －－ 北京：文物出版社，2024.4
ISBN 978－7－5010－8367－1

Ⅰ．①万… Ⅱ．①深… Ⅲ．①历史文物－中国－明代
－图录 Ⅳ．① K871.452

中国国家版本馆 CIP 数据核字 (2024) 第 048500 号

萬曆那些年
万 历 文 物 主 题 特 展

编　　者：深圳市南山博物馆

责任编辑：崔　华　智　朴

责任印制：张道奇

出版发行：文物出版社

社　　址：北京市东城区东直门内北小街 2 号楼

邮　　编：100007

网　　址：http://www.wenwu.com

经　　销：新华书店

装帧设计：雅昌（深圳）设计中心　王展彤

印　　制：雅昌文化（集团）有限公司

开　　本：889mm×1194mm　1/16

印　　张：14.25

版　　次：2024 年 4 月第 1 版

印　　次：2024 年 4 月第 1 次印刷

书　　号：ISBN 978－7－5010－8367－1

定　　价：320.00 元